Lorna Chaplin first visited the Cyclades island of Paros in 1979 on a two-week package holiday and fell in love with it at once. Return visits were limited while she completed her nursing training but Paros has been her home since February 1984 where she and her cats have now been joined by the man who came to fix the television aerial two years ago.

> To Jeanie (Emonson) with love
> and congratulations.

About this book

Having extensively used travel guides within Greece and South East Asia, I have tried to include in this book the things I have often wished were in those on which I have previously depended.

I have substituted historical data and descriptions of church interiors with explanations of how to find hotels, post offices etc. in the belief that those visitors with a keen interest in archaeology or old churches will probably buy one of the specialist books on these subjects.

It is meant as no insult to the readers' intelligence that I have, where possible, recommended eating places. Of course part of the fun of a holiday is to wander at leisure around the towns and villages and find a favourite taverna; but on your first day perhaps a little travel weary, you may be grateful for some suggestions.

If you speak the language then finding things presents no problem, but Greek as a second language is rare; hence the directions under useful addresses.

The language chapter is meant to help only in emergencies and is no substitute for a phrase book. Apart from place names, all Greek words have been spelt phonetically. The accent denotes the syllable to be stressed.

Prices, hotel names and standards can change almost overnight. Last year's supermarket can be this year's boutique, *taverna* or disco. Successive editions will endeavour to keep all information as up-to-date and accurate as possible.

Have a great time!

Acknowledgements

The author would like to thank Marketousa and Nikos Tamigos (Maria Tours, Santorini), Andonis Fostieris (Amorgos), Andonis Sideris (Folegandros), the President and Yeorgos Kavanaros of Kimolos, Manolis Loudaros (Anafi), Maria Maouni (Paros).

With special thanks to Ann Coleman and Dr Margaret Kenna whose help was as invaluable as their company was enjoyable.

Last and by no means least, to Kostas in appreciation of all the hours he spent on ferries to keep me company at the weekends.

Front Cover: The sheltered, sandy cove at Vathi (Sifnos) can be reached only by caique from the port. The islanders will tell you there is a path but it is neither indicated by signpost nor marked by the wear of footsteps.

Greek Island Series
Ios, Santorini
and the South East Cyclades

Lorna Chaplin

Amorgos · Anafi · Kimolos · Sifnos
Sikinos · Folegandros · Milos

Roger Lascelles, Cartographic and Travel Publisher
47 York Road, Brentford, Middlesex TW8 0QP Telephone: 01-847 0935

Publication Data

Title	Ios, Santorini and the South East Cyclades
Typeface	Phototypeset in Compugraphic Times
Photographs	Lorna Chaplin (unless otherwise indicated)
Maps	Joyplan, Chessington, Surrey
Index	Jane Thomas
Printing	Kelso Graphics, Kelso, Scotland.
ISBN	0 903909 68 5
Edition	This first, May 1989
Publisher	Roger Lascelles
	47 York Road, Brentford, Middlesex, TW8 0QP.
Copyright	Lorna Chaplin

All rights reserved. Other than brief extracts for purposes of review no part of this publication may be produced in any form without the written consent of the publisher and copyright owner.

Distribution

Africa:	South Africa —	Faradawn, Box 17161, Hillbrow 2038
Americas:	Canada —	International Travel Maps & Books, P.O. Box 2290, Vancouver BC V6B 3W5
	U.S.A. —	Boerum Hill Books, P.O. Box 286, Times Plaza Station, Brooklyn, NY 1121T, (718-624 4000)
Asia:	Hong Kong —	The Book Society, G.P.O. Box 7804, Hong Kong 5-241901
	India —	English Book Store, 17-L Connaught Circus/P.O. Box 328, New Delhi 110 001
	Singapore —	Graham Brash Pte Ltd., 36-C Prinsep St.
Australasia	Australia —	Rex Publications, 413 Pacific Highway, Artarmon NSW 2064. 428 3566
Europe:	Belgium —	Brussels - Peuples et Continents
	Germany —	Available through major booksellers with good foreign travel sections
	GB/Ireland —	Available through all booksellers with good foreign travel sections.
	Italy —	Libreria dell'Automobile, Milano
	Netherlands —	Nilsson & Lamm BV, Weesp
	Denmark —	Copenhagen - Arnold Busck, G.E.C. Gad, Boghallen, G.E.C. Gad
	Finland —	Helsinki — Akateeminen Kirjakauppa
	Norway —	Oslo - Arne Gimnes/J.G. Tanum
	Sweden —	Stockholm/Esselte, Akademi Bokhandel, Fritzes, Hedengrens. Gothenburg/Gumperts, Esselte. Lund/Gleerupska
	Switzerland —	Basel/Bider: Berne/Atlas; Geneve/Artou; Lausanne/Artou: Zurich/Travel Bookshop

Contents

Part 1: Planning Your Holiday

Part 2: The South East Cycladic Islands

Appendices

Index

ONE

Introducing the Greek Islands

No matter where you live in Britain, whether it be in a depressingly grim industrial area or a quaint rural village, the Greek islands are so different, so "un-British". There are islands where it is possible to imagine an advertising company having designed every feature in such a style as would make it most appealing to visitors. Tiny white sugar cubes have shutters and doors painted all the colours of the rainbow side by side with flaming geraniums and bougainvilia to make the brightest display. There's higgledy piggledy town planning with mazes of winding streets containing picture postcard courtyards and balconies; grey flagstones with the joins painstakingly whitewashed and here and there a magnificent forsythia or clematis springing from the tiniest cracks between them; harbours and shorelines dotted with little fishing boats lovingly painted in the most brilliant colours by their proud owners, who can be seen at sunset tenderising octopus on the rocks before hanging them up to dry.

The street displays of the shops rival that of any Eastern bazaar and the cries can be heard of the traders who peddle fruit, vegetables and fish from baskets attached to the saddles of enigmatic looking donkeys; road traffic consists of octogenarians riding donkeys and mules, overtaken by the ever-so-slightly faster drivers of rotovator engines attached to their two wheeled carts.

Fields of impossibly red poppies and sunkissed daisies inspire even those who have never before looked twice at a wild flower; here are rolling hills, rocky mountains with a house, chapel or monastery gouged seemingly inaccessibly into them; dry stone walls, ramshackle farm buildings, goitre-necked cattle, indignant turkeys, skittish sheep and vociferous farm dogs.

The pace of life and attitude to it are summarised by the custom of asking anyone seen looking at their watch if they are taking antibiotics. What other reason could you have for needing to know what time it is!

How fresh seems the enthusiasm on the faces of the dancers who are lured to the floor by the bazouki music, like sailors to the sirens; the generosity and hospitality of anyone whose threshhold you cross. How the conversations full of shouting and gesticulating contrast with the unearthly quiet of siesta time. Get the picture? It is just gloriously different!

Greece has facilities to suit all holiday requirements but if your criterion is to have everything the same as back home with sunshine to go with it, then probably the smaller islands would be wasted on you. Spanish resorts have adequate supplies of English fish and chips, English tea, English pubs (apologies to the Welsh and Scots) — and I for one hope it never happens to the Greek Islands.

The South East Cycladic Islands

The Cyclades Islands lie to the south east of the southern tip of mainland Greece and are so named because they are arranged in a rough circle. Of the twenty-eight islands in this group, two-thirds are inhabited. Of the south eastern islands covered by this book, only Antimilos and Polivos are uncolonised although the maps show many other tiny islets, all meticulously named and most of which have had a solitary church built on the highest point.

Amorgos
This is an island that is much loved by its visitors, who return year after year, declining other islands with either more facilities or more solitude; perhaps for them Amorgos has the ideal balance between the two. The two halves of the island offer a different appeal and although there are more hotels and beaches in the north, the south attracts more visitors — which delights the remarkably friendly villagers.

Anafi
Totally uncommercialised and therefore offering very little in the way of facilities, the island has many attractive beaches and enough tavernas to cater for all who seek a relaxing holiday.

Folegandros
This is a rocky island with few beaches but a delightful capital and exceptionally friendly people. An ideal place to 'get away from it all' and enjoy the bonhomie that prevails among visitors who soon become acquainted in the little restaurants or music bar.

Ios

Ios is small in size but as packed with facilities as it is with tourists. The "party" island is a very popular destination for those who wish to soak up the sun on idyllic beaches, the inexpensive booze in the numerous bars, and favourite sounds in the (almost) all-night discos.

Kimolos

Another totally uncommercialised island with only one small village — which is only partially occupied — Kimolos has a few beaches, fifty rooms to rent and some attractive walks for those who want to get away from *absolutely* everything.

Milos

Surprisingly this island receives only a moderate number of tourists even though the only interruptions to sandy beaches along its coastline are other features of interest including sea-caves, lunar-like rocks and a pirates' lair. Milos is a large and attractive island that offers a diversity of facilities to its visitors.

Santorini

There is only one Santorini and everyone should visit it at least once in their lifetime. The volcanic landscape is breath-taking and the highly developed tourist industry has been controlled to leave areas where the traditional lifestyle can be appreciated. It's a comparatively expensive island that has facilities for doing almost anything that takes your fancy.

Sifnos

Sifnos is a green and beautiful island with very picturesque villages and landscapes. Commercialisation is well under way and enough facilities exist to provide a little of everything. The island is renowned for its ceramics produced by hand in family owned workshops.

Sikinos

There is a small and barren island whose solitude is ideal for those who enjoy walking and swimming from rocks. The island's only village is a charming example of a typical, unspoilt Greek community.

Official information

The National Tourist Office of Greece (N.T.O.G.) Known in Greece as E.O.T. (pronounced like yacht), this organisation is generally helpful and friendly. The British branch is at 195/197 Regent Street, London W1R 8DR. Nearest underground stations Oxford Circus and Piccadilly Circus.

The bulky pamphlet *General Information about Greece* is packed with facts, figures and relevant data that cover most queries. Specific to the Cyclades is a fourteen-page leaflet with many colour illustrations that gives hotel details and a brief summary of each island including all those covered in this book.

Offices on the Greek mainland relevant to this book are at:
— Piraeus: 105, Vassilissis Sofias Str.
— Athens: East Main Airport, Eliniko
— Athens: National Bank of Greece, 1 Karageorgi Servias Street. The latter is on a corner of Syntagma Square in Athens and has an enquiry desk where the multilingual staff are equipped with numerous handouts, maps and brochures which cover most enquiries. They produce a weekly summarised boat timetable of departures from Piraeus which can be invaluable.

A new information desk has been opened to try to shorten the length of the queues in the National Bank. It is situated within the General Bank on the corner of Ermou Street in Syntagma Square. This facility is open from 08.00 to 20.00 hrs Monday to Friday and from 09.00 to 13.30 on Saturdays, closed Sundays year round.

Tourist police There used to be a separate tourist police force equipped with armbands bearing the flags of the countries whose language they spoke. Although signs marked 'Tourist Police Station' are still the thing to look for, these are mostly now within the regular police offices where an officer is available to deal with any complaints or queries and dispense leaflets and maps to visitors. Some of them even speak a language other than Greek!

Passports Visitors to Greece require a valid passport. The various stages of Common Market membership are changing the visa regulations but it has not been possible to obtain precise information about the new regulations and their implementation, either from consulates in Athens or London. The local police stations are carrying on as before concerning the renewal of visas, and passports are still stamped on entry and exit from Greece. Nationals of other countries are advised to check with NTOG or the Greek embassy whether there are any special visa or permit conditions which might affect them.

Island	Nautical miles from Piraeus	Airport	Telephone dialing code	Hotels	Camping ground	Water shortage	Night-life	Sandy beaches	Motor bike hire	Car hire	Petrol supply	Official port of entry for yachts
Amorgos	138	NO	0285	YES	YES	MODERATE	SOME	SOME	YES	NO	NO	NO
Anafi	145	NO	0286	NO	NO	DESPERATE	JUST	MANY	NO	NO	NO	NO
Folegandros	93	NO	0286	YES	YES	MODERATE	SOME	FEW	NO	NO	NO	NO
Ios	111	NO	0286	YES	YES	DESPERATE	LUNATIC PROPORTIONS	PLENTY	YES	NO	NO	NO
Kimolos	88	NO	0287	NO	NO	MILD	JUST	FEW	NO	NO	NO	NO
Milos	87	YES	0287	YES	NO	VERY MILD	MODERATE	IN ABUNDANCE	YES	YES	YES	YES
Santorini	130	YES	0286	YES	YES	DESPERATE	PLENTY	MANY	YES	YES	YES	YES
Sifnos	79	NO	0284	YES	YES	MILD	MODERATE	PLENTY	YES	NO	YES	NO
Sikinos	113	NO	0286	NO	NO	VERY MILD	JUST	FEW	NO	NO	NO	NO

Island facilities at a glance

TWO

When to go

Between November and March the weather is very unpredictable, days of gales and torrential rain alternate with sunny blue skies and warm breezes so gentle that the sea is mirror-like.

The locals think it unwise to swim in the sea before Easter, at which time it will have been pleasantly hot for at least a month. Little old ladies in their multilayered black widow's weeds will touch your bare sun bronzed arm and enquire with a look of disbelief, "Surely you are cold!" Heaven help you if you get hayfever or sneeze in their presence, it sprouts "I told you so" looks!

From April to October the sun can be pretty much relied upon to make cooling off in the sea necessary, although it rarely gets uncomfortably hot in the shade.

In July and August the *sirroco*, a warm but energetic wind from North Africa, can make trying to eat outside in the evening rather interesting! It usually lasts for three days at a time and alternates with a *meltemi,* a northerly wind that is generally cooler but less strong.

All meteorological details given are those issued by the station on the Cycladic Island of Naxos.

Average monthly atmospheric air temperatures in C°						
	Jan	Feb	Mar	Apr	May	Jun
max	14.6	15.0	16.0	18.9	22.2	25.7
min	9.5	9.3	10.3	12.7	15.6	19.5
	Jul	Aug	Sept	Oct	Nov	Dec
max	27.0	27.1	24.9	22.3	19.6	16.3
min	21.8	22.0	19.8	17.0	14.0	11.4

Average temperatures of sea surface in C° at 14.00 hours

Jan	Feb	Mar	Apr	May	Jun
15.0	14.9	15.1	16.8	19.1	22.2

Jul	Aug	Sep	Oct	Nov	Dec
23.9	23.5	22.7	20.0	17.4	15.5

Average number of days rain

Jan	Feb	Mar	Apr	May	Jun
15.4	11.0	10.1	6.8	4.2	2.1

Jul	Aug	Sep	Oct	Nov	Dec
0.5	0.5	2.2	6.8	8.3	14.1

The sea temperature seems to vary from beach to beach and of course the hotter you get, the colder the sea feels!

All ferries, no matter how large, do not sail in winds of force 9 (and sometimes 8) on the Beaufort scale. These gales can spring up within hours and so beware! — plans including last minute sailings to the mainland may leave you stuck on the island while your flight leaves Athens without you.

The area of sea between Naxos and Amorgos is particularly vulnerable to gales and it may be impossible for ferries to leave from these islands even when sailings are permitted from the ports on other more westerly islands.

Where a choice of spelling of island and town names exists, I have opted for that most closely resembling the form used on the island itself. In most cases, the main town has the same name as the island itself but the locals and bus timetables nearly always use the word Hora or Xora in place of the normal name. Many travel guides spell this word as Chora having explained somewhere in the volume that the Greek letter X is pronounced as the ch in the Scottish word loch. But having seen the locals struggle with my surname until it is turned into Kaplin or Tsaplin, I can't see the sense in this!

THREE

Getting there

Milos and Santorini are the only two islands described in this book which have airports, and it is not possible to fly into either of them direct from the UK on a scheduled flight. (But see chapter 17 for information about international charter flights into Santorini.) Both airports are connected to **Athens** airport by Olympic Airways domestic flights.

All the islands covered in this book may be reached by ferry, either from **Piraeus** on the Greek mainland or by way of one of the other islands. This chapter aims to help prospective travellers decide on which is the best means for them of reaching the Greek mainland — the first lap of their journey — and once there, to continue on to the island or islands of their choice.

By air to the Greek mainland

The country's main airport is in Athens and although there is a second airport in Thessaloniki to the north, it is unlikely that any of you would use the weekly flight there from London as it is a lot farther away from all the ports.

The airport is situated ten kilometres south of the centre of Athens and the main buildings are divided into what are known as the east main airport and the west main airport — but both use the same runways. The west main airport is used exclusively by Olympic Airways, the Greek national airline, for both overseas and domestic flights. The east main airport is used by all airlines except Olympic.

There are frequent daily flights from both London's Heathrow and Gatwick airports with most of the charter and more inexpensive flights from the latter.

Unless you plan to visit any of the nine islands with one of the holiday companies that cover them, your enquiries will be for flight-only details from your local travel agent or from the agencies listed in the low price travel magazines sold in large newsagents.

To enter Greece in this way, regulations demand that you have an accommodation voucher. The companies that sell flight-only seats will provide you with such a voucher for a token payment (e.g. £2). When you receive your tickets, the wallet will also include a confirmation of booking at an address within the mainland. You are not expected to use this address and could find that it is a derelict building if you try to do so.

The flight from London takes approximately three and a half hours and most of the charter flights are at night which are timed nicely to get you to the port in time to watch the sunrise over the docks and then catch the first ferry of the day. Of course you may wish to spend some time on the mainland before moving on but it would really be wiser to plan to see the Acropolis etc. at the end of your holiday; thus if bad weather delays your sailing from the last island at least you would not miss your return flight home.

By rail to the Greek mainland

Greece can be reached by rail from most European countries. From England the cost is surprisingly high and greatly exceeds that of the average budget flight even for those under 26 years of age or who hold a student card. There are daily departures from London's Victoria Station for Athens. A typical journey departs 14.30 hours Monday and arrives at 08.40 hours Thursday having changed trains at Paris and Venice. Under 26's are eligible for the Eurorail card that entitles you to unlimited travel on any of Europe's railways for one month.

I have heard many tales of long delays at the borders and of harassment by customs officials and, except for Eurorail card users, it would seem that the only advantage in this form of transport is for those who hate flying.

By coach to the Greek mainland

I have used this form of travel on ten occasions and with two different companies. If I were to give the details here, it would be understandable if many of you thought the book had turned into a disaster novel at this point! Probably some passengers actually do have an uneventful journey but it hasn't happened to me yet.

Suffice it to say that meals at the stopping places en route are exorbitantly expensive and that the length of time drivers are willing to spend at toilet stops is quite inadequate (e.g. 5 minutes where there is one toilet and 40 + passengers); so best to take plenty of low fibre food and have a urinary catheter inserted for the three day (they say!) journey! Some drivers will not permit food on board so disguise it.

This is by far the cheapest form of travel to Greece. Details of prices and how to book can be found in the travel and entertainment magazines. One of the companies now claims to be licensed. You should be aware that a company of this type went bankrupt a few years ago. Of course there are some more reputable firms operating from London to Central Europe but these do not cover Greece. So if ever you book with them to Athens, you may find the second half of your journey is with one of the infamous companies. The reverse is true and on a return journey, I found myself the object of disdain by the driver and courier on the respectable service when they realised who our tickets were with.

A good tip is to take your towel and toiletries onto the ferry where there is a hot shower in the toilets on the upper deck; especially welcome on the return journey.

By road to the Greek mainland

There is no real difficulty in driving across Europe to Greece. The easiest route uses the new toll motorway through Austria from Salzburg to Klagenfurt. The main *autoput* (M1/E94-E5) through Yugoslavia is joined near Ljubljana. It is a flat and uninteresting road crowded with international juggernauts; much has now been reconstructed to full motorway standards, and new sections are regularly added; but parts of the remainder are in dangerously poor condition, especially north of Belgrade. That stretch can be bypassed by taking the M3 south west from Maribor through Osijek to join a good section of the *autoput* near Sremska Mitrovica — a slower but safer and more interesting route.

The coast road down the Adriatic is even more interesting, but 300 kms longer. Being slow and winding, it is also somewhat dangerous. It is not at present possible to transit through Albania, and for political reasons there have sometimes been restrictions on foreign motorists in the province of Kosovo.

Fuel coupons can be bought at the Yugoslav border, for payment in foreign currency. Regulations seem to change in detail from year to year; only recently did it cease to be compulsory for foreigners to use coupons to buy fuel. Currently each coupon has a nominal value of 1300 dinars, but entitles the motorist to an additional 10 per cent of fuel at standard prices (a complex procedure about which some pump attendants feign ignorance). Unused coupons can be refunded at a border, or through the Automobile Association of Yugoslavia (AMSJ) in Belgrade.

The easier way of getting to Greece is to drive down through Italy and take one of the many car ferries listed above. Those sailing from ports in the 'heel' of Italy (Apulia) should give the cheapest overall journey.

Documentation A 'Carnet de Passage en Douanes' is not necessary for periods of up to four months in Greece: instead, an entry is made in the driver's passport at the frontier. Even after four months, a banker's guarantee is an acceptable alternative to the 'Carnet'. An International Driving Permit is not needed by holders of British and several other European national driving licences. But an insurance 'Green Card', valid for Greece, is mandatory. Entry into Greece will be refused if a passport contains the stamp of the Turkish Republic of Cyprus (Kibris).

Fuel prices The price of Super (96 octane), 80dr/litre, is comparable with other countries in the area, Regular seems significantly cheaper, but has the very low octane value of 90. Diesel at 38dr/litre, is cheap. There is no price discounting, although fuel prices do vary marginally within the country, depending on distance from the refinery. Currently there is no petrol coupons scheme for tourists.

Motorways The 'motorway' network, classified as National Road, extends from Evzoni on the Yugoslav border to Thessaloniki and Athens, and from Athens to Patras. The greater part is still single carriageway, although some upgrading work is in progress on busier sections. Some stretches of unimproved main road remain. Driving standards are relaxed, although by convention slower-moving traffic drives on the hard shoulder of single carriageways. Between Evzoni and Athens there are at present three toll sections — although another near Thessaloniki can be expected before long — the first near Katerini, and two between Athens and Patras. Charges seem modest to foreigners — for example, about £1 for a private car between Evzoni and Athens. Tickets need to be retained for authentication within each toll section.

Road signs On main roads the road signs invariably appear in pairs. The first shows place names using the Greek alphabet, and is followed at about 100m by a second in the roman alphabet. Numerals of course present no difficulty. All other road signs conform generally to normal European conventions. Turnings off towards camp sites are almost always signposted from the main road.

Breakdowns The Automobile and Touring Club of Greece (ELPA) operates a breakdown service in less remote parts of the country, which is free to foreigners who are members of their own national Automobile or Touring Club. Assistance is obtained by dialling 104.

By ship to the Greek mainland

Most of the remaining international passenger ships calling at Greek ports now operate as cruise liners. Virtually the only exceptions are ships run by the Russian Black Sea Company, a few of which call at Piraeus. Thus by far the greater part of passenger capacity now depends on ubiquitous drive-on/drive-off car ferries. Scheduled services, some sensitive to the Near East political situation, give the following possibilities:

from	between	duration	frequency
Cyprus	Limassol to Piraeus	31-65 hrs	at least weekly
Egypt	Alexandria to Piraeus	35-37 hrs	weekly
Israel	Haifa to Piraeus	45-59 hrs	several weekly
Italy	Ancona to Igoumenitsa	23-25 hrs	at least daily
	Ancona to Patras	33-36 hrs	at least daily
	Bari to Igoumenitsa	12-14 hrs	daily
	Bari to Patras	18 hrs	daily
	Brindisi to Igoumenitsa	9-10 hrs	several daily
	Brindisi to Patras	15-19 hrs	several daily
	Otranto to Igoumenitsa	9 hrs	several weekly
	Venice to Piraeus	39-40 hrs	at least weekly
Syria	Latakia to Piraeus	78 hrs	occasional
	Tartous to Volos	(?)	weekly
Yugoslavia	Bar to Igoumenitsa	16 hrs	2 x weekly
	Dubrovnik to Igoumenitsa	17 hrs	2 x weekly

Piraeus Ever since the ancient Greeks abandoned their primitive arrangements on Phaleron beach, Piraeus has been the chief port of Athens. It has two harbours: the main harbour, used by all international and domestic passenger ships and car ferries; and Zea, which serves practically all the hydrofoils.

The following services connect Piraeus with Athens:

— The *elektrikos* railway, for city centre and north east suburbs, whose terminal is near the north end of the waterfront.

— The Peloponnese main line railway, from whose terminus just north of the *elektrikos,* some dozen trains a day leave for the Peloponnese via Athens (Peloponissou) station.

— Various buses. Most originate from the bus terminal in Karaiskaki Square, beside the main shipping company offices, and 200m south of the *elektrikos* terminus. Green bus 040 has its own terminal on Sakhtouri street, between Zea harbour and the international passenger terminal on the main harbour. The following buses go direct to the airport (east): yellow express bus from Akti Tselepi (which is the south side of the main shipping offices block on Karaiskaki Square), stopping at the west airport on the way; and blue bus 101 from Klissovis Street/Theotaki. The following go direct to the airport (west): yellow express bus from Akti Tselepi (see above); and blue buses 107 and 109 from Klissovis Street/Theotaki, towards the end of the residential peninsula (probably not a convenient pick-up point for tourists, but there are intermediate stops en route).

To travel between the main harbour and Zea, take blue bus 905 from outside the *elektrikos* station, leaving every 15 minutes. Alight at Platia Freatidas, whence the hydrofoil berths can be seen a short distance below.

Air transport in the Aegean

Only two of the islands covered by this book have airports: Milos and Santorini. **Milos** receives only domestic flights which use 19-seater propellor-driven aircraft for the 45-minute flight from Athens. There are two flights per day all the year round, and in season the morning and evening departures are boosted by a midday service three times per week.

Santorini has a larger airport and the service from Athens uses 30-seater aircraft. In summer there are departures to: Athens (3 a day), Mykonos (1 daily), Rhodes (4 a week) and Crete (3 a week). (See also chapter 17.)

The smaller aircraft are as prone to cancellation on windy days as the ferries and the fact that you have successfully taken off from Athens does not necessarily mean that you will land at Milos; it is far from rare for aircraft to be forced to return to the mainland having unsuccessfully tried to land in cross winds. If you make enough of a nuisance of yourself you may be able to get a seat on one of the flights once the weather has cleared.

Domestic departures at Athens are from the west main airport where, (facing the terminal building) the departments are, from left to right, domestic arrivals, domestic departures, international arrivals and international departures. The check-in desks have a list of islands above them which seem to be for decorative purposes only. Go to the desk with the shortest queue and take note of where the clerk says you should be.

Your boarding card will have on it the departure gate number and although the various waiting areas have indicator boards above them, your flight may leave without its details ever having been displayed. When a stewardess appears at the appropriate door, go up and show her your boarding pass until you get an affirmative answer. This is the only way to ensure that you don't get left behind!

Getting to the west main airport

● From east main airport, Express Bus No. 19 every 30 minutes from 06.00 to 24.00 hours, fare 100 drachmas, and from 24.00 to 06.00 hours every 90 minutes, fare 150 drachmas. Olympic Airways Shuttle Bus, hourly departures.

● From central Athens, Express A and B from Syntagma Square 06.00 to 24.00 hours every 20 minutes, fare 100 drachmas, and hourly from 24.00 to 06.00 hours, fare 150 drachmas. Bus No. 133 from Othonos Street in Syntagma Square from 05.40 to 24.00 hours every 20 minutes, fare 30 drachmas. Bus No. 122 from Vas. Olgas Avenue, 05.30 to 23.30 hours ever 15 minutes, fare 30 drachmas. Night Bus No. 167 from Akademias Street off Syntagma Square approximately hourly from 00.30 to 04.00 hours.

● From Piraeus, Express Line Bus No. 19, 06.00 to 24.00 hours every 30 minutes, fare 100 drachmas and 24.00 to 06.00 hours every 90 minutes, fare 150 drachmas.

A bit of gesticulating gets the point across much better and how can you sit in a café without discussing the politics of the day?

Sea transport in the Aegean

The only justified criticism of Greek ferry boats is the difficulty in getting accurate information about them. Many shipping companies operate mainland to island services and all are realistic enough to reject the idea of a seasonal timetable. The ships have a habit of occasional over enthusiastic docking which necessitates a month or two in dry dock and juggling with the schedules. (This is a good reason for not standing at the end of the jetty while your ferry comes in!)

The vessels vary in age and size but the majority are large car ferries some of which are ex cross-channel ferries. The service to Milos, Kimolos and Sifnos includes smaller vessels that can hold up to twenty vehicles. The larger ships have four classes of passenger in the summer, while in winter everyone buys a third class ticket and sits in the tourist class lounge.

— First class: The standard varies from boat to boat but you are generally paying for seclusion. The fare is about four times that of third class and where there is the choice, works out dearer than flying the same route.

— Second class: Upholstered bench type seats which are comfortable for a snooze. Twice the fare of third class.

— Tourist class: "Pullman" (coach type, reclining) seats in long rows. 50 per cent more expensive than third class.

— Third class: On deck! There are slatted wooden seats and open areas for sunbathing but the decks are grubby and you need something to lie on. (See Sunburn page 52) A few boats have a small lounge for third class passengers. Bear in mind that it gets very cold on board after the sun sets, if you are on a long journey.

Ticket offices On the mainland, particularly in Piraeus, there is always a choice of ticket offices *(practórios)*. Each office represents one or more shipping companies and will deny all knowledge of other companies' sailings. So ask at least three before concluding which is the first departure. Never phrase the question, "Is there a boat to Sifnos tonight?" — the answer will always be in the affirmative as it is obviously what you want to hear. Just ask when the next ferry leaves for Sifnos. Prices don't vary from one office to the next but you may be sold a second class ticket if you don't specify. It is possible to buy tickets on board but you never know if someone will be checking them as you get on. There seems to be no pattern to it. Tickets for vehicles are always needed before embarkation. The service using the smaller ships that visit Milos, Kimolos and Sifnos has tickets available on board at 20 per cent lower than the shore rates but this is risky: there may still be someone checking tickets before you embark, and being sent back to find the agent may mean that the ship sails without you.

Food All the large boats have a restaurant in the second class lounge for the use of all categories of passengers. The food is of reasonable quality and price. However you can't guarantee them opening for evening meals. In the tourist class lounge is a snack bar that sells coffee, beer, soft drinks, snacks, hot pizzas and toast. One of the ferries has the restaurant in the lounge which is not a good idea either for those who are hungry or those who are feeling a bit nauseated.

Other facilities Cabins can be reserved when you buy your ticket but they get full quickly in summer and are suffocatingly hot and stuffy.

You can sometimes change money and travellers cheques at the purser's office, especially if you haven't yet bought a ticket or can point out that you need it to pay for a hot meal; but you would be ill-advised to depend on this.

Despite the fact that most of the men on the islands seem to have spent some time as crew on merchant vessels, the Greeks on the whole are the world's worst sailors and the paper bags start fulfilling their function even before the ship has left port! You may want to bring ear plugs and blindfold if you find the plight of your fellow passengers contagious! For the same reason, the toilets start off in immaculate condition at the beginning of the journey but rapidly deteriorate.

Some ships show videos in the tourist lounge but you have to be sitting near the television to hear the soundtrack as the Greeks rely on the subtitles which can be read from a distance.

Departure ports

Piraeus
The country's main port is easily reached from both the centre of Athens and the airport. Not surprisingly it is not a very attractive area and the overall impression is of "grey".

The National Tourist Organisation of Greece prints a free weekly sailing timetable for all ports which can be obtained from their desk in the National Bank of Greece at Syntagma Square or at the east main airport. Because of the size of the port, it is essential to know where your ferry leaves from. Ask when buying your ticket or at the tourist police office inside the electric train station. Chondrocoucis inside the station is the only one I have found that handles all the shipping companies. They speak excellent English and are very helpful.

Along the main road, parallel to the dock, are banks, souvenir shops, cafés and *tavernas*. Inside the wire-fenced area of the docks on the corner of the row of ticket offices, is a café that leaves chairs outside all night, thus providing somewhere to wait and watch the sun rise if you have arrived early from a night flight.

Transport to Piraeus is fairly good — the journey takes less than an hour.

● From east and west main airports, Express Line Bus number 19 every 30 minutes from 06.00 to 24.00 hours, fare 100 drachmas, and every 90 minutes from 24.00 to 06.00 hours, fare 150 drachmas. The bus makes three stops within the port area, the third of which, Akti Tzelepi, is the nearest to the usual berths of the ferries serving the islands covered in this book.

● From central Athens, Green Bus No. 40 from Filellinon Street (off Syntagma Square) every 10 minutes, 24 hours service.

● By electric train from Monastiraki, Thission or Omonia stations in Athens. Trains run every five minutes from 05.00 to 24.00 hours. If you can't find the station, say "traino" to someone and look lost. Omonia station is down the escalators in the square and is not a particularly safe place to go after dark. Train fare 30 drachmas. (See Chapter 8, Transport.)

● From Peloponnisou and Larissis railway stations, Yellow Trolley Bus No. 1 to Amalias Avenue in Syntagma Square. From 05.00 to 24.00 hours every 10 minutes, fare 30 drachmas. See above for details of the second leg of the journey from central Athens. The alternative is to take the Express Bus B or Ḅ to the airport and then the Express Line No. 19 to Piraeus but this is such a long way round I can't imagine anyone wanting to do it.

Rafina

A much more appealing port than Piraeus, it is often suggested that choosing this as a departure point (if you have the option) saves time and money on fares. However these benefits are usually lost in the process of getting there!

● From the airports, you have to take a bus or taxi to the centre of Athens and then walk or take a taxi (if you can get one) to

Mavromateon Street at Areos Park, and it is a thirty minute walk.
● From Athens at 29 Mavromateon Street on Areos Park, Orange
Buses leave every 45 minutes from 05.50 to 22.00 hours and more
frequently in rush hours on the hour long journey. Luggage goes in
the compartment at the side of the bus. Fare 140 drachmas paid
inside the bus.

Island hopping possibilities

The general structure of passenger shipping in the South East
Cyclades has already been discussed, and further details are given
in Part 2 under the individual islands. But many readers will be
interested in planning journeys to other Greek islands by scheduled
ferries. Reliable information about some of these is hard to come
by, even in Greece. The NTOG issues a weekly sheet covering
sailings from all ports. *Greek Travel Pages* and the *Key Travel
Guide* can be helpful, but neither is comprehensive. Nor are layout
and information easy to understand. The three-monthly paper
Journey to Greece contains a detailed list of departures from, and
maps of, 21 islands, including all those covered by this book except
Sikinos. It is sold on some of the ferries as well as in the souvenir
shops.

Nevertheless virtually all the islands of any importance now have
a car ferry service, relied on as the chief means of bringing in goods,
as well as for transporting foot passengers. A few passenger-only
ships remain, but the tendency is for them to be replaced by car
ferries or hydrofoils. Another trend is for some of the ferries
operating from the Athens area to move away from the congestion
of Piraeus to smaller ports elsewhere — sometimes also shortening
distances.

Where islands lie close to one another, in relation to their distance
from the mainland, fairly logical networks have evolved within these
groups. But intending passengers should be aware of the following
factors:
● The islanders themselves have usually little interest in visiting
other islands. Instead they wish to get to the mainland as quickly
as possible. This requirement is, of course, opposite to that of the
island-hopping tourist, but has had more influence in the planning
of schedules.
● With few exceptions, local operators show little interest in
publicising their services. Schedules, where found, probably list

sailings by ship rather than the operating company. Destinations are given as ports, sometimes with obscure names, rather than islands.

● Shipping companies, all of them privately owned, have their route licences reviewed annually by the Ministry of Mercantile Marine. Whilst established companies are unlikely to be disturbed, more marginal operators bidding for fringe routes may have little idea until late in the previous year which, if any, they are going to be allocated. Bankruptcies, leading to the unexpected halting of services, are not uncommon.

● Modern ferries are required to conform to specifications making them suitable for troop-carrying duties in emergency — the evacuation of PLO fighters from Tripoli in 1983 for example. Hence the apparently casual attitude to passenger comfort in some cases.

● Services between certain Greek islands and the Turkish mainland are very sensitive to tension between the two countries. Sailings may not actually cease, but operators can keep a very low profile — even in departure ports reliable information can be exceptionally hard to obtain. In any event, fares are *very* high in relation to the distances involved; inward and outward bound prices can also vary.

The information contained in the table on following pages has been assembled to assist in the planning of economical island-hopping sequences. It covers only car ferry services; naturally foot passengers, who are free to travel by passenger ships, hydrofoils and caiques, enjoy additional mobility. Islands not listed are either too small, or else motor vehicles cannot be landed there.

Under each island the following information is shown: island ports liable to be given as destinations; normal mainland departure ports; journey times; maximum weekly frequencies; other islands which can be reached directly, as first port of call; international connections. Naturally, since the underlying data are continually changing, confirmation must be obtained locally.

The following example will help to make things clear:

Chios (Eastern Aegean group). Alternative port on the island, Mesta. Mainland departures from Piraeus, 10 hours, more than 7 sailings each week; Kavala, 16 hours, 1 sailing each week; and Thessaloniki, 16 hours, 1 sailing each week. From Chios there are direct sailings to Lesbos, 4 hours, more than 7 each week; and to Samos, 3 hours, 2 each week; Psara, 4½ hours, 4 each week; and Dinoussa, 1¾ hours, 6 each week. There is an international connection to Cesme, 1 hour, more than 7 each week.

Key to table

CY = Cyclades. DO = Dodecanese. E = East Aegean. IO = Ionian.
N = North Aegean. SA = Saronic. SP = Sporades.

Numbers in brackets are the approximate duration of journey in hours of the quickest journey. Other numbers are for frequency in high season, whilst f indicates at least 7 services each week. ? indicates there are some doubts as to reliability of data, although some connection is thought probable.

Island destination	Mainland departure	Other islands reached directly	International connections
Aegina (SA) (Ag Marina)	Piraeus (1) f Methana (¾) f	Poros (1¾) f	
Alonissos (SP)	Volos (5½) f Ag. Konstan- dinos (6) 3 Kimi (2½) 3	Skopelos (½) f	
Amorgos (CY) (Egiali: north) (Katapola: south)	Piraeus (11-16) 4	Koufonissia (1) 1 Paros (4½) 1 Astipalea (3) Donoussa (1½) 4	
Anafi (CY)	Piraeus (14) 2	Santorini (1) 2 Crete (?) 2	
Andros (CY) (Gavrion)	Rafina (3) 6	Tinos (2½) 6	
Antikythira	Piraeus (18) 2 Gythion (7) 2	Kythira (1) 2 Crete (3) 2	
Astipalea (CY)	Piraeus (?) 2	Amorgos (3) 1 Donoussa (3½) 1 Kalymnos (?) 1	
Chios (E) (Mesta)	Piraeus (10) f Kavala (16) 1 Thessaloniki (16) 1	Lesbos (4) f Samos (3) 2 Psara (4½) 4 Dinoussa (1¾) 6	Cesme (1) f
Corfu (IO) (Kerkyra)	Igoumenitsa (1½) f Patras (11½) f	Paxi (2) 3	Brindisi (8) f Bar (13) 2 Bari (10) 6 Dubrovnik (15) 4 Otranto (7) 5+

Island destination	Mainland departure	Other islands reached directly	International connections

Crete
  Chania
  Heraklion
  Kastelli
  Sitia
	Piraeus (11) f
	Piraeus (11½) f
	Gythion (4) 2
	Kassos (3) 2?
		Shinoussa (7) 1
		Naxos (8) 2
		Antikythira (3) 2
		Anafi (?) 2
			Limassol (27) 2
			Haifa (43) 2

Donoussa (CY)	Piraeus (?) 4	Amorgos (1½) 4 Astipalea (3½) 1 Naxos (2) 1	
Folegandros (CY)	Piraeus (10-15)	Sikinos (1) 1 Milos (1) 1 Santorini (3) 3	
Ikaria (E) (Ag. Kirikos) (Evdilos))	Piraeus (10) f	Syros (?) 1 Paros (4½) 2 Samos (2) f	
Ios (CY)	Piraeus (9) f	Naxos (2) f Santorini (2) 2 Paros (2) 2 Sikinos (?) 2	
Ithaka (IO) (Vathy) (Frikes)	Patras (6) f Astakos (2) f Vassiliki	Kefallonia (1) f Paxi (5) 1	
Kalymnos (DO)	Piraeus (14) f	Kos (2) f Leros (1½) 5 Astipalea (?) 1	
Karpathos (DO)		Kassos (1) 2? Khalki (3) 2?	
Kassos (CO) Kea (CY)	Crete (3) 2? Karpathos (1) 2? Lavrion (1) f	 Kythnos (2) 3	
Kefallonia (IO) (Poros) (Sami) (Fiskardo)	Killini (1½) f ?Patras (3½) f Igoumenitsa (5) 3 Vassiliki (1½) f Astakos (3½) f	Ithaka (1) f Zakinthos (2) 1	Brindisi (14) 3
Khalki (DO)		Karpathos (3) 2? Rhodes (3) 2?	

Island destination	Mainland departure	Other islands reached directly	International connections
Kimolos (CY)	Piraeus (11) 4	Milos (2) 2 Sifnos (2) 2 Syros (4) 1	
Kos (DO)	Piraeus (16) f	Kalymnos (2) 6 Rhodes (4½) 6 Nissiros (?) 1	Bodrum (1½) ?
Koufonissia (CY)	Piraeus (13) 2	Schinoussa (1) 1 Amorgos (1) 1	
Kythira (Ag. Pelagia) (Kapsali) (Platia Ammos)	Piraeus (11) 2 Neapolis (1) 5 Gythion (2½) 2	Nil	
Kythnos (CY)	Lavrion (2) 3 Piraeus (3½) 4	Serifos (2) 4 Kea (2) 3	
Lemnos (E) (Myrina) (Kastro)	Kavala (5) 4 Piraeus (?) 1 Ag.K'standinos (10) 1 Kimi (5½) 1	Lesbos (6) f Ag. Efstratios (2) 2	
Leros (DO)	Piraeus (12) 5	Kalymnos (1½) 5 Patmos (1½) 5	
Lesbos (E) (Mytilini)	Kavala (14) 2 Piraeus (13) f Thessaloniki (16) 1	Chios (4) f Lemnos (6) f	Dikeli (2) ?
Milos (CY)	Piraeus (11) 5	Kimolos (2) 2 Sifnos (2) 4 Syros (4) 1	
Mykonos (CY)	Piraeus (7) 5 Rafina (6) f	Tinos (?) f? Delos (1) f	
Naxos (CY)	Piraeus (8) f Rafina (7) f	Ios (2) f Iraklia (1) 1 Paros (1) f	
Nissiros (DO)	Piraeus (?) 1	Kos (?) 1 Tilos (?) 1	(?cars landed?)
Oinoussa (E)		Chios (1¾) 6	

Island destination	Mainland departure	Other islands reached directly	International connections
Paros (CY)	Piraeus (6) f Rafina (5½) f	Syros (2) f Naxos (1) f Ios (2) 1 Ikaria (4½) 2 Amorgos (4½) 1	
Patmos (DO)	Piraeus (10) 5	Leros (1½) 5 Syros (?) 1	
Paxi (IO)	Patras (10) 1	Corfu (2) 3 Ithaca (5) 1	
Poros (SA)	Methana (½) f Piraeus (3) f Galatas (5 mins) f	Aegina (1¾) f	
Psara (E)		Chios (4½) 4	
Rhodes (DO)	Piraeus (15 +) f	Khalki (3) 2? Kos (4½) 6 Symi (?) 1	Limassol (14) 4 Marmaris (2) Latakia (55) 1 Haifa (28) 1 Alexandria (39) 1
Salamis (SA)	Perama (10 mins) f Perama (Megara) (¼) f	Nil	
Samos (E) (Vathy) (Karlovasi)	Piraeus (12) f	Ikaria (2) f Chios (3) 2	Kusadasi (2) f
Samothraki (N) Karala (4) 1	Alexandrou- polis (3) f	Nil	
Santorini (CY) (Athinios) (Oia)	Piraeus (10) f	Ios (2) 2 Anafi (1) 2 Folegandros (3) 3	
Schinoussa (CY)	Piraeus (13) 2	Iraklia (½) 1 Koufonissia (1) 1	
Serifos	Piraeus (5) 5	Kythnos (1½) 5 Sifnos (2) 5	

Island destination	Mainland departure	Other islands reached directly	International connections
Sifnos (CY)	Piraeus (7) 5	Milos (3) 5 Serifos (2) 5 Kimolos (2) 2	
Sikinos (CY)	Piraeus (13) 3	Ios (?) 2 Folegandros (1) 1	(No cars landed)
Skopelos (SP)	Volos (4) f Ag. K'dinos (4) f Kimi (3½) 3	Alonissos (½) f Skiathos (1) f	
Symi (DO)	Piraeus (?) 1	Tilos (?) 1 Rhodes (?) 1 Patmos (?) 1	
Syros (CY)	Piraeus (4½) f Rafina (3½) 3	Ikaria (4½) 1 Kimolos (4) 1 Paros (2) f Tinos (1) f	Milos (4) 1
Thassos (N) (Prinos)	Kavala (1) f Keramoti (½) f	Nil	
Thera (CY) (Santorini) (Oia)	Piraeus (12) 5	Anafi (2) 1 Ios (3) 4 Folegandros (3) 1	
Tilos (DO)	Piraeus (?) 1	Nissiros (?) 1 Symi (?) 1	(?cars landed?)
Tinos (CY)	Rafina (5½) f Piraeus (6) f	Andros (2½) 6 Mykonos (1) f Syros (1) 4	
Zakinthos (IO)	Killini (1) f	Kefallonia (2) 1	

Note. Euboea and Levkas, both technically islands, but with bridge or chain-ferry road connection, have been treated as if part of the mainland

FOUR

Accommodation

All the islands have a variety of accommodation available, to be found predominantly in the main town and to a lesser extent the other centres of population. Names of hotels with category, telephone number and location are listed in the individual island chapters.

What to expect

The local tourist police and N.T.O.G. allocate a category for all rooms to let both in private houses and hotels. This is decided by the standard and amount of facilities available. Something like a telephone in the room can upgrade it from a C to a B. The standard varies from one island to another and of the islands covered by this book, Santorini and Ios are the most expensive; but to put it in proportion, this means paying about an extra £3 per night there.

One characteristic of Greek rooms is that they are smaller than you may be used to and although the furniture is kept to a minimum it is often necessary to organise a one-way system around the room! Another is that the sheets seem to have been carefully measured to exactly fit the top of the bed with no allowance for tucking in at the bottom, top or sides! If you are used to more than one pillow, improvisation is called for.

Conventional baths are about as rare in Greece as Turks, and showers are the norm. Some islands experience a shortage of water in the summer and many water heating systems use solar panels, which means that your shower will be hotter at night than in the morning. Some have electrical back-up for the winter and the controls look like a fuse box with a round knob bearing "O" and "I" symbols. You may be allowed to turn on the water heater yourself but many Greeks seem to believe that these controls are beyond the understanding of most tourists! Towels and soap are provided.

The room category and basic and extras charges are shown on an official card usually displayed behind the door. The prices shown are the maximum the owner is allowed to charge by law but if business is slack he may be willing to accept less. If the room charge does not include the price of showers, this will also be shown on the card, so look here for otherwise hidden extras. The various categories are: Luxury, A, B, C, D and E.

On most of the islands, people meet the ferries and cries of "Rooms, rooms" indicate their purpose. This practice is illegal but tolerated. The hotel and room representatives judge the new arrival by his/her appearance and approach those they think most suited to their accommodation. Many establishments run mini buses to transport you from the port to your room.

Camping

It is strictly illegal to sleep on beaches with or without camping equipment but, except for town beaches, the police turn a blind eye until prompted into action by local hotel and room owners. If all official accommodation becomes full (as it can) then sleeping under the stars is permitted as long as no fire of any kind is started either deliberately or accidentally. If you do start a fire, you are automatically provided with free accommodation for a minimum of two months in a Greek prison!

Camping grounds are a rarity and seldom meet the demand. The authorities are now providing financial aid to those who plan to build camp sites but as they require a large plot of land and must have a high standard of facilities, they are still a costly venture.

FIVE

Food, drink and leisure activities

Food and where to eat

Most people will have eaten in a Greek restaurant in their home country at least once. If you have ever ordered *mezedes* you will have a good idea of the character of Greek food as it consists of a little of most of the dishes on the menu. Because most of the Greek restaurants in the U.K. are Cypriot owned, there will be slight variations in flavourings and of course the selection may be more limited by the difficulty in obtaining fresh ingredients, such as octopus and squid, which are readily available in Greece.

One major difference however will be the temperature of the food. In Greece it is unusual to find dishes served hotter than warm. This is not due to poor service or lack of facilities but is the way Greek people are used to serving and eating their food.

Centuries ago, each village had a central kitchen where the food was prepared for the entire community and a member of each family would take the appropriate containers to the kitchen and return with the family's share of the food at meal times. On the way home, the food would cool considerably and this is said to be the reason why they developed the habit of eating luke-warm meals.

Because not many Greek kitchens have an oven, just hot plates, you can often see the women taking containers of food ready for cooking to the bakers shop where, for a small fee, their cakes or joint of meat are cooked for them.

Breakfast The Greek people do not place much importance on breakfast and the N.T.O.G. is at present encouraging hotels to offer an alternative to the "continental breakfast" that consists of tea or coffee, toast, butter, jam and sometimes a piece of madeira cake.

Many cafés advertise "English breakfast"; however, if you choose sausages with your eggs, you will find them very "un-English" and more like little spicy frankfurters, tasty nevertheless.

The ham is rather like salami but the bacon is what we are used to and of a high quality.

Most cafés use evaporated milk in coffee which is always called "Nescafé" to distinguish it from Greek coffee (it will be instant, though not necessarily that particular brand). Also, you can expect to have hot milk to go with your morning cup of tea! The butter is unsalted and the apricot marmalade bears a striking resemblance to apricot jam (delicious).

Tavernas
They vary in standard and prices but generally serve inexpensive traditional dishes which you select by going into the kitchen and pointing at what you want. This is an excellent way of ensuring that you like the look of what you order and of overcoming any language problems, although most owners and waiters speak at least enough English to cover all eventualities in their work. Only a very few *tavernas* serve desserts or coffee and you are expected to go elsewhere for "afters".

Restaurants
Their main difference from *tavernas* is that they are open at lunch time as well as in the evening and generally have a larger selection of food that may include steaks and some French and English dishes. They may also provide a small selection of desserts, coffee and after dinner drinks.

Zaharoplastéons
These cake shops sell gateaux, pastries and yoghourt to eat on the premises or take away. Coffee, tea, soft drinks, liqueurs and spirits are served but never wine or beer. It is to these shops you come for the sweet course of your meal and after dinner drinks. They generally keep shop hours.

Cafeniós
All types of alcohol, soft and hot drinks are sold with a small selection of cakes.

Ouzerías
The Greek men (especially those whose working life is over) spend a large part of each day in a café or *ouzeria* watching the world go by or discussing politics, emphasising each point with energetic hand gestures and raised voices. The latter is often confused by foreigners as a sign of a heated row in progress but this doesn't follow in

Greece. A friendly but enthusiastic conversation can often include the participants yelling at each other!

On offer you will find Nescafé and Greek coffee, *ouzo, Metaxa* cognac, beer, soft drinks and a few pastries. If you order *ouzo* or cognac, be sure to order some *mezes* which complement the drinks. They are small plates of tomato, cucumber, bread with *tsatsiki, taramasalata* and anchovies and, of course, olives. At about forty drachmas, it is also excellent value.

If you are watching the sunset from one of these establishments, you will be able to enjoy some of the grilled octopus that is served at this time of day. The octopus have to be tenderised which explains why people can be seen apparently taking out a bad temper on the unresisting (lifeless) octopus. They are hung up to dry in the sun so watch your head as you walk under the awnings! Small pieces of the grilled tentacles are served on sticks with lemon juice and it is customary to drink the remaining juice from the saucer, it is also the best bit in my opinion! Don't be put off by its appearance, it is delicious.

Octopi drying in the sun, after being beaten to tenderise them.

Menus

A popular source of tourist entertainment are the bilingual menus found in all eating places. The variety of spelling mistakes can be hilarious and it is occasionally impossible to work out what they are trying to say. I can recommend "roast staff" from a *taverna* in Syros. Presumably one of the waiters fell foul of the chef! (Perhaps you would like to send me any howlers you find for inclusion in future editions).

Although the menus are lengthy, only the dishes with prices beside them are available. The two prices for each dish are with and without tax. It is usual to leave a 10% tip divided between the waiter and boy who brought the bread and drinks.

Meat When you look at the dishes on offer in the kitchen, the meat will probably look as if it died of old age and has been dried out even more in the cooking. Don't you believe it! If the cook can manage to get it on to the plate before it disintegrates, you will see how deceptive appearances can be.

Fish and shell fish   In fish tavernas you choose your fish from a refrigerated display cabinet and it is then cooked for you. Price is by weight and is not as cheap as you might expect.

Drinks

Greek coffee This is similar to Turkish coffee but I don't suggest you order it as such. It comes with varying amounts of sugar and is always served black in a *demi-tasse* with a glass of cold water. Never stir it and beware of the considerable amount of sediment in the bottom. You drink it: without sugar — *skéto;* with a little sugar — *médrio;* incredibly sweet — *gleekó.*

Retsina Wine containers used to be made of hide treated with tree sap or resin. This flavoured the contents and the Greeks developed a taste for it this way and so today they add resin to some of the many local wines purely for the taste. This is definitely an acquired taste but at 100 drachmas a bottle, some feel the incentive to acquire it!

When drinking any alcoholic beverage in Greece, it is customary to chink glasses before drinking and with each refill. The origin of this custom is said to be that the Gods decreed that wine should please all five senses. The only one not obviously satisfied was hearing, hence chinking glasses.

Wine Those of you who enjoy being able to expound on which end of which vineyard the grapes came from for each glass of vintage French wine, may be a little disappointed in the Greek wines. Very few if any eating places on the islands covered stock imported wines although there can be a large selection of the local produce. My own preference is for the rosé wines but I have never been noted for having a refined palate.

Beer At least four different brands of beer are sold in Greece. *Fix* is a local brew and *Amstel* is produced in Greece under licence from Holland. They are all lager type beers and are sold by the litre. Bottle sizes are half litre which is roughly three quarters of a pint for 100 drachmas. Draught lager is new to the islands but catching on fast.

Ouzo An aniseed flavoured spirit that is clear until water is added at which time it turns a milky white.

Cognac Locally produced brandies are slightly sweeter than those produced in France but are enjoyable and at 70 drachmas a time, very inexpensive. Duty free bottled five star Greek brandy works out at a ludicrous £3.00 for 750 mls.

Raki Sometimes known as *souma* this colourless spirit is very popular with the locals. The taste and more particularly the aroma varies greatly. One I tried had such a revolting smell that try as I might, I couldn't get it near enough to taste it.

Drink (and food) prices are all dictated by the tourist police who consider the facilities available before setting the price, e.g. beer is always 100 drachmas in a *cafenión* but may be 200 drachmas in a bar and 300 in a discotheque. The local businessmen on my home island of Paros recently went on strike for two days bemoaning the price fixing level. It hasn't made any difference however and they lost £50,000 per day in takings.

The Greeks never seem to suffer the day after a heavy drinking session and this is probably due to the fact that large glasses of cold water are served with all spirits and they never drink without taking a little food at the same time.

Entertainment

The variety of nightlife on each island is of course proportional to the extent of its involvement in the tourist industry.

Discotheques

These places vary greatly from an improvised dance floor in the middle of a field to fairly sophisticated night spots. The disc jockeys seemed to be picked for fairness of face rather than musical knowledge or technique and generally have a complete disregard for whether anyone else is enjoying the music. Not all discotheques have an admission charge but where they do, it will include the price of your first drink. The cheapest way to get round the higher drink prices is to buy a bottle of wine and share it.

Bars

In summer, most bars have seats outside where it is possible to talk above the music played.

Bazoukis

There is never an admission charge but the price of drinks can be phenomenal, e.g. 1000 drachmas for a gin and tonic. Some *bazoukis* only serve whisky to drink and most have a large selection of food including the speciality of fruit salad — popular since it is usually the cheapest thing on the menu. Live Greek music is played by a group of at least six musicians and one or more of them will sing. The locals tend to get very enthusiastic on an evening at the *bazouki* and the plates inevitably start being shattered on the dance floor as a gesture of appreciation.

Greek dancing

I don't think it is possible not to enjoy watching the local men dancing, at least on the first occasion. Whether it is a single old timer dancing because he just can't help himself or a group of young lads out to impress the girls, you can't help being caught up in the atmosphere it creates and the skill involved. By all means clap along to the music but lone females should realise the significance of crouching at the edge of the dance floor and clapping on their own to a male dancing, as in some places it implies a very intimate relationship. You might prefer to watch the dancing in a bar or disco rather than a *bazouki* where it tends to get too crowded to be able to see what is happening. Many bars have someone used to teaching tourists the steps and they have a strange knack of conveying what you are supposed to do next even if not in words.

Manolis Arvanitis surrounded by the vats that contain some excellent wines at his cellars in Akrotiri, Santorini.

Cinemas

Many islands have open air cinemas that add an extra dimension to watching old movies. Most films shown in the summer are in English with Greek subtitles. Comedies are less suitable than thrillers or westerns as the locals often read the subtitles and start laughing, preventing you from hearing the punch line in the dialogue.

Sailing

Ios is the only island covered that has sailing boats for hire but it may be possible to make arrangements to hire privately owned vessels from locals or resident expatriates.

Flotilla holidays There are a small number of mainland companies which organise flotilla holidays. The selection of islands to be visited is often decided by the consensus of opinion among the passengers; and so you may see a large number of sailing boats moored in the harbour. Be warned that they can be moored there for six months or more as, in the past, the island port police have declared the boats to carry inadequate safety equipment and have impounded them for eventual auction to cover the mooring fees and fines. This of course left the unfortunate holidaymakers stranded, so check out the company first if you plan to use this method of getting about.

Swimming

One of the joys of the beaches is that swimming is safe for both adults and children, as undercurrents and undersea shelves are very rare indeed. Swimming is an enjoyable part of most people's holiday both because of the need to cool off intermittently when sunbathing and because the Aegean has an enticing variety of all the shades of blue and green imaginable, that proves irresistible to young and old alike. Many beaches are bordered by rocky outcrops where snorkellers can explore the variety of marine life found there.

In the shallows, if you stay still long enough, tiny transparen fish, with markings on the tail that look like eyes at the other end, will gently nibble at your legs possibly to remove the grains of salt that the evaporating seawater leaves.

Beaches

Most Greek beaches are thoroughly cleared of seaweed and litter at the start of the season. One of the reasons why sleeping on the beaches is opposed is because of the human waste and rubbish that has been left there to spoil the enjoyment of others in the past. Enough said.

Santorini and Ios have windsurfers and water skiing equipment for hire and tuition from their most popular beaches.

Nudism

The Greek people do not understand the joys of swimming and sunbathing naked or even topless. On my home island, the locals have been prompted into printing notices reminding people that it is illegal and suggesting where they should go to prevent causing offence. Where idiotic individuals have been callous enough to peel off on town beaches, you will find mothers feel obliged to take an alternative route home with school children.

All the islands have at least one beach suitable for nudism so it is no hardship to show some consideration for your hosts. Many holidays have been spoilt when offenders were taken to court, fined and had their passports endorsed to prevent subsequent re-entry to the country. The police have been known to don swimming trunks and to look for naturists before returning in uniform to make the arrests.

Diving

A new law has been introduced that forbids the use of air tanks for diving unless a permit is held by the diver. This is to prevent the removal of antiquities and damage to unexcavated archaeological sites on the sea bottom.

The multitudinous colours of the souvenir shops' wares rival those of any oriental bazaar and many bargains can be found.

SIX

Shopping

There are few things that cost significantly more in Greece to make it worth bringing them from home. Photographic film is marginally cheaper at home and black and white film is almost impossible to find in Greece. If you plan to be self-catering, beef stock cubes, coffee whitener and bran are about the only things not available at the supermarkets. Double the cost in Greece are paperback books, and I consequently enter a plea on behalf of Greek island resident expatriates who would dearly love to get their hands on some fresh reading material: don't throw books and newspapers away, try and find someone to give them to or persuade your hotel to start a small library.

Shop opening hours

Like all the times quoted in this chapter, these must be taken as a guide only, but in general they are 08.00 to 13.00 hours and 17.00 to 20.00 hours Monday to Saturday, with no evening opening on Mondays and Wednesdays. There have been many strikes lately by shop employees protesting at the opening hours. When they eventually won their case there were further strikes to have the hours changed back again. The winter opening hours currently in use are Mondays 13.00 to 19.00 hours, Tuesdays to Saturdays 09.00 to 19.00 hours, closed all day on Sundays. Souvenir shops and boutiques may not bother to close in the afternoon and may be open on Sundays and late into the evening depending on the number of potential buyers on the streets. Most shops close for the various religious holidays and in addition to these, shops have their own name days according to the type of shop. No warning is posted, even in Greek, of these holidays to enable you to stock up on food, or other things you might need.

This father and son team have an open shop for those who want to see the production of the famous Sifnos ceramics.

What to buy

Everyone has different ideas about which souvenirs are tasteful or gaudy but Greece has a large selection of the former. Practical cheesecloth dresses, attractive ceramics, handmade jewellery, fringed scarves, dazzling posters and postcards, leather shoes, brassware and statuettes are just some of the souvenirs that are worth buying for reasons other than purely as a holiday memento. Particular bargains are: Greek cigarettes, cognac, wines, suntan oil, cheesecloth dresses and silver jewellery.

Comparative sizes
● Shoe sizes

English	3	4	5	6	7	8	9	10	11
Greek	35½	37	38	39½	40½	42	43	44	45½

● Bust sizes

English	32	34	36	38	40	42	44
Greek	81	86	91	97	102	107	112

● Dress sizes

English	8	10	12	14	16	18
Greek	36	38	40	42	44	46

Weight

Almost everything in Greece is sold by weight in kilos, including string, wine, paper and nails: 1 kilo = 2.2 lb.

Banks and currency

Banks

Only Sifnos, Milos, Ios and Santorini have banks but all the islands have post offices (see p.49). If you have an account with a Greek bank then you must withdraw enough money to cover visits to the smaller islands (cheque books are not issued).

If you plan to stay in Greece longer than three months, save the pink exchange slips as you will need them when applying for a visa renewal.

Opening hours are from 08.00 to 14.00 hours (13.30 Friday) Monday to Friday. Where a large number of tourists are found, the banks may stay open later and may even open on Saturdays for exchange only. These hours will be displayed outside the bank. Some Greek banks have been on strike on and off for the last three years but an exchange desk remains open.

Currency

The exchange rate for sterling varies from day to day. Currently (January 1989) £1 = 267 drachmas. The amount of drachmas you can buy in your home country and re-exchange after the holiday is regulated by Greek law. Any British bank will be able to provide up-to-date details before your departure and also order the appropriate amount of drachmas if you wish to have some cash ready for your arrival in Greece.

There are also regulations that demand that large amounts of imported foreign currency be declared at your port of arrival. The current amount is always displayed inside the airport, passenger transfer buses and other conspicuous places near immigration desks but it is usually higher than the amount the average holidaymaker would bring so doesn't normally create a problem. If you are bringing a substantial amount of sterling into Greece then it is definitely wiser to join the endless queue to the tiny office that provides absolutely no privacy in which to display your wealth to the customs official. If for any reason you still have over the legal limit when leaving Greece and are unlucky enough to have it found on your person at the port of departure, it may be impounded.

Bank Notes These come in increasing size according to value, and in various colours. Denominations are: 50 drachmas (light blue); 100 drachmas (pinky red); 500 drachmas (green); 1,000 drachmas (brown); and 5,000 drachmas (navy).

The newly introduced 5,000 drachma notes are very difficult to change and if you offer one to pay for a packet of cigarettes, the shopkeeper might well become hysterical. On the subject of shopkeepers, it is easier to understand their being reluctant to give change when you realise that Greek banks will not provide bags of coins.

Coins These are also in increasing size according to value. Denominations are: one drachma (bronze); two drachmas (bronze); five drachmas (silver); ten drachmas (silver); twenty drachmas (silver); and fifty drachmas (silver).

The fifty drachma coins are new and, although larger, can be easily confused with the twenty drachma coin, so be careful.

Supermarket prices may have two figures after a decimal point. This is because the drachma is theoretically divided into a hundred lepta. No lepta coins exist and this is just a way of inching up prices.

Kiosks

Found on most street corners these orangy brown painted constructions are known as *peripteros* in Greek. Somehow they manage to stock a larger selection of goods than most Woolworths, including cigarettes, matches, sweets, nuts, chocolate, razors, pens, contraceptives, aspirins, vapour rub, throat sweets, newspapers, books, magazines, maps, adhesive tape, paper, envelopes and a multitude of other things. Most have a metered telephone for public use.

The occupants are often disabled or war veterans as kiosks are State allocated. Opening hours vary but many only close from midnight to 07.00 hours.

(Opposite) *Fisherman tenderising an octopus by dashing its lifeless body against the jetty. (Klima, Milos)*

Post offices

Post offices *(Taheedroméeo)* are easily distinguished by their bright yellow sign posts with black lettering. The same colour scheme is found on the post boxes. Opening hours are from 07.30 to 14.15 hours, larger branches may stay open for an additional half hour; closed Saturdays and Sundays. All post offices on the smaller islands and the main post office on the larger islands provide a Poste Restante service. Passports must be presented when collecting letters and parcels. There may be some confusion over which letter of the Greek alphabet your post has been filed under, so ask anyone writing to you to use only your Christian and surname and to underline the surname. This avoids the possibility of it being filed under Mr or Mrs.

Postage stamps can sometimes be bought at shops selling postcards. They are allowed to charge 10% above the face value of the stamps.

Post offices now also undertake all foreign exchange transactions, which is very useful on the smaller islands that don't have banks. In peak season the smaller offices may run out of drachmas as the float is insufficient to cope with large numbers of people wishing to exchange cheques or cash drachmas.

Opening a post office account in Athens is an ideal way of avoiding having to transport all your cash from island to island. Passports are always needed when making withdrawals.

Books and newspapers

Very few of the islands covered by this book stock English paperbacks or newspapers. Where available, newspapers from home are priced according to their weight and the published price of the paper: 150 to 300 drachmas. Some glossy magazines are available on some of the more commercialised islands but you can expect to pay as much as you would for a fairly thick novel at home.

(Opposite) *This tiny church in Vathi (Sifnos) is decked with flags on its name-day.*

Telephone offices

The abbreviation for the Greek name for these offices is O.T.E. pronounced owtay. Every island has at least one but they vary from large buildings to someone's spare room! International calls and local calls can be made from here but local calls are not allowed from the O.T.E.'s in Athens, you must use a kiosk.

The 'phone booth contains a meter and a table to tell you the cost of various meter readings, e.g. 100 units = 600 drachmas. The length of time for each unit depends, of course, on where you are calling. Before dialling, the meter must be at zero. The assortment of noises made by the telephone system is very different from ours. The ringing tone at first sounds like our engaged tone but the notes are coupled and have a long pause between couples.

When your call is completed, you pay at the desk having indicated which booth you have used. A receipt will be given. Opening hours 08.00 to 14.30 hours and 17.30 to 21.00 hours Monday to Friday, half day only Saturday; but these hours vary enormously from island to island.

Transfer charge and person to person calls will be placed for you but it may entail waiting in the office for up to two hours. These offices also handle **telegrams** but it is always cheaper to telephone.

Telephone kiosks

Kiosks with blue or orange bands at the top of the sides. The blue ones use ten drachma coins which must be inserted before dialling but after lifting the receiver. The orange booths can take international calls and use ten, twenty and 50 drachma coins. A tiny dim red light goes on a split second before you get cut off and there are no pips to tell you to put in more money. Unused coins should be returned to you when you replace the receiver but this system is as prone to faults as our own. None of the kiosks takes incoming calls. Very little vandalism of 'phone boxes is found in Greece.

The kiosks known as *peripteros* (see page 48) have metered 'phones from where you can make local or international calls but enquire about the cost of a ten-unit call before you begin, as some owners illegally charge much more per unit than the official rate. A local call that uses one unit is always slightly more expensive than a tenth of a ten-unit call charge.

SEVEN

Your health and comfort

General health

It is not necessary to have any inoculations before visiting Greece unless you have recently visited an area where yellow fever or cholera are endemic.

The main health problem you may encounter is from the laxative properties of the olive oil, which forms an ingredient for almost everything except bread! A change of diet has the same effect, so don't rush to the chemist for antibiotics at the first sign of gastric disturbances. A kaolin mixture or Lomotil taken after each bowel movement gives speedy relief and can be purchased from local chemists without prescription. Remember to maintain an adequate fluid and salt intake or you could get some painful stomach cramps.

Medical care

All of the islands covered by this book have at least one doctor. On smaller islands, the doctor is probably newly trained and doing a form of community work in lieu of his National Service. The location of surgeries is mentioned under the Useful Addresses section of each island chapter. In some places the surgeries double as the only pharmacy. Opening hours are posted outside. In case of serious illness, patients are transported by boat or helicopter to the nearest hospital.

Theoretically if you obtain form E.111 from an office of the Department of Health and Social Security (see leaflet S.A.30) before leaving the U.K., you will be entitled to treatment at a token cost. In practice, the problems of getting the necessary forms completed by the doctor make this a nonsense. A consultation will cost approximately 2,000 drachmas.

Medical insurance

Medical insurance to cover accidents and emergency treatments is recommended for travellers to Greece. Remember that there are few hospitals in the islands and should you need hospital treatment the costs of being transported there — even apart from the treatment itself — could be very high indeed. Your travel agent will give you the latest information about insurance policies. Check that the sum you are insured for is adequate. Emergency surgery such as an appendectomy, for example, can be very costly. If you were unfortunate to need anything like this, it would also delay your return home — so make sure that the medical insurance you take out is realistic.

Hazards

Greece is the home of a few nasties including small white scorpions, black widow and brown hermit spiders plus two species of poisonous snakes. You are extremely unlikely to encounter any of these little treasures whose venom is rarely fatal. Should you be unlucky enough to be bitten or stung, don't try to imitate anything you may have seen in the movies as this only speeds up the spread of the venom. Get help as quickly as possible giving a description of what "got you".

There are no strong currents or undercurrents on the island beaches and the only hazards are sea urchins and jellyfish, both of which are painful. Leave sea urchin spines alone, trying to get them out only pushes them further in. Apply some olive oil and keep pressure off the affected area, they will work their own way out. Jellyfish can sting even when dead and beached, so if you find one why not move it out of harm's way with a stick, as other people may not be as observant as you.

Sunburn

There is one very serious danger lurking for the unprotected: the sun. The gentle breeze is very pleasant but it masks the strength of the sun. This is particularly true on the sundecks of the ferries, where you can relax comfortably for long enough to start your holiday with third degree burns. Sun screens and after-sun creams are available more cheaply than at home and with a mind-boggling selection. Take sunbathing slowly at first. Whatever you do, never fall asleep in the sun.

Toilets

Greek toilets are not the sort of places in which you would want to spend any length of time. Most are of the type we are used to but some are the "squatting" variety. In the latter be careful of losing the contents of your pockets. In all toilets, a basket or bin is provided into which you must put all used toilet paper as the plumbing can't cope with it. To operate the flush, push the plunger underneath the cistern.

Men's and women's toilets are differentiated by the usual trousered and skirted figures on the doors. A single toilet usually bears the letters "W.C.".

Public toilets are rare but all eating places have to have them by law. Only a few will insist that they are for the use of customers only. The Greek word for toilet is pronounced *too allétta*.

Drinking water

The water is safe to drink in all parts of Greece but the taste varies. On Syros it is very briny and fresh water is sold by street vendors. Bottled water is available at all supermarkets for about 35 drachmas for 1½ litres. These plastic bottles are useful for taking to the beach (and light to bring back to town for disposal!).

The water generally has a high concentration of minerals and a photographer friend tells me that he finds it impossible to get any of his developing chemicals to dissolve in it.

EIGHT

Getting about

Time and distance

Greek time is one or two hours ahead of that in England depending on the time of year. This is not the only difference, as the whole concept of time bears no similarity to our own. Expressions such as morning, midday, afternoon and evening are so flexible as to be meaningless. If you are trying to make an appointment of any kind, specify the exact hour and even then, unless you say "English time", rendezvous will be anything up to two hours later or "Greek time".

Distance is equally flexible and "near", "just around the corner" and "a few minutes walk" can turn out to be a few kilometres.

Transport

Taxis In the centre of Athens it is very difficult to get a taxi even though these bright yellow cars account for about 50% of the traffic. The problem is caused by the regulations introduced to lessen smog in the city, which stipulate that vehicles may only be used on alternate days according to the registration numbers. Consequently car owners must find an alternative method of getting to work — and they appropriate the taxis.

Taxi ranks at Syntagma Square, underground stations and both airports are some good places to try. Otherwise you have to stand somewhere where the occupied taxis are forced to slow down or stop, traffic lights for example, and shout your destination through the window. Each passenger will pay the full fare unless you are travelling together therefore picking up single passengers rather than a couple is more lucrative.

On all of the islands, the taxis are metallic grey.

Buses On the smaller islands, buses have a relaxed atmosphere and it doesn't matter which door you use to get in. On the mainland the pace of life is that much faster and you have to get in at the front and pay the exact fare into a box near the driver. If you don't know the fare, have plenty of change handy. Keep the ticket as many routes are checked on every journey by an inspector.

There is no uniformity in the appearance of bus stop signs and so you just have to watch where people get on.

On the islands, all the buses are a mid blue unless otherwise stated.

Trains Operating only in Athens and its suburbs, is a single route electric train. These trains mostly run above ground from Kifissia to Piraeus and are useful for getting from Athens to Piraeus. The fare is 30 drachmas. Ticket offices don't open until about 08.00 and so if the man in the office is ignoring you, just walk through the turnstile and tickets will not be checked at the other end. Later in the day you must buy a valid ticket from either the machines or office and retain it for inspection at the other end.

Pedestrians Crossing the road in Athens takes either nerves of steel or suicidal tendencies. They have plenty of red and green men to advise you but the trouble is that when the green man is lit, it only means that traffic wishing to go straight ahead is being shown a red light. Where drivers can turn right, they may still have a green light and so you have to dodge them.

There seems to be no penalty for parking on the zebra crossing while waiting for the lights to change and you often have to pick your way around and squeeze between vehicles on the striped area.

Motorbike and moped rental

The majority of the bikes have seen better days and survived some rough treatment that the mechanics have a knack of camouflaging with a coat of paint. Some important points to remember when hiring a vehicle:-

● Make sure it works! Take it for a test drive which will also —
● Ensure that you can handle it.
● Negotiate the price, especially if hiring for more than one day. Does the price include petrol?
● Get the 'phone number of the agency in case of breakdown. All of them have their own breakdown trucks and they don't sit idle for long.

● Seriously consider asking for one of their crash helmets. At no extra charge, these look like multi-coloured tortoises and while they won't do a thing to improve your image they may prove to be your salvation: there are so many "holidaydrivers" around in the summer that even if *you* know what you are doing, you may fall foul of someone else who doesn't. Accidents are literally an everyday occurrence. Most people get away with cuts and bruises but every time you see that helicopter overhead, someone has been badly injured and is on his way to the hospital.

● Make a firm arrangement about returning the bike. The expression used may be "for the day" but if you return a bike after 19.00 hours, you will find yourself unpopular with the employee who has had to work late for you. If you want to keep it until the next morning, make it clear.

● Be sure you take notice of the traffic signs (the same as in Europe). Many of the roads are closed to motorbikes and mopeds even though cars are permitted. Keep your eyes open and don't forget that they drive on the right hand side in Greece!

● Where island roads are of a poor standard, choose a bike with large wheels.

● Resist the temptation to take corners at speed.

If your bike does break down and your knowledge of their mechanical workings is limited or non-existent, try taking the petrol cap off and then rocking the bike from side to side to hear if you have got any petrol left (petrol = *vin zeé nee)*. Have a look for the sparkplug which is usually found between the front wheel (that round thing) and a grooved thing the size of a small loaf of bread that burns your fingers when you touch it. If you locate the sparkplug make sure that there is a cap sitting firmly on top of it rather than waving about in the air on the end of its cable. If you can't find the sparkplug, see if you can spot a hole where one used to be, and then walk back and look for it.

Remember it is illegal to drive motorised bikes through towns between the hours of 13.00 and 17.00 or indeed to make any loud noise.

Car hire

Only Santorini, Sifnos and Milos have vehicles for rent at the moment. Details from the tourist offices.

NINE

Customs and things you should know

Worry beads

Most Greek men have at least one set of worry beads which they produce at moments of tension, boredom or relaxation. These can be made of metal, plastic or wood and do not, as might be suspected derive from the rosary (in fact some scholars say that the rosary derives from them . . .) Some men are very adept at making the beads fly up and down their fingers and techniques vary. You will not see women using worry beads.

Drinking

As mentioned in Chapter Five, each refilled glass should be chinked with those of your companions. There are a variety of salutations used and as these can be rather confusing, just repeat whatever your host says.

Gestures — and avoiding trouble

One gesture that can be very confusing is the one used to indicate a negative reply to a question. The head is tipped sharply back and may be accompanied by a clicking noise made with the tongue. This gesture can be modified until only an eyebrow is moved almost imperceptibly and it takes a while to get used to it — you tend to think that either they haven't heard the question at all or are asking you to repeat or explain it.

The Greeks have a hand gesture that is far worse than our reversed victory sign in its meaning. To hold up your hand at eye level with fingers spread and palm outwards at someone is the worst possible insult and virtually a challenge to a duel. Even worse is to use two hands! I couldn't understand the look of horror on someone's face when I tried to use sign language to convey that I would be back in ten minutes by pointing to my watch and then holding up the appropriate number of fingers!

The word *malláka* is used frequently in conversation by Greek males and is the derogatory name for someone who satisfies their own physical desires. This is always used light-heartedly (there are far worse for when they are serious) but it is never acceptable for foreigners to use this word no matter how close you are or how long you have known somebody.

The evil eye

The Greek people believe strongly in the power of the evil eye — which is thought to be put on anyone who causes another to be envious of them. The way to avoid it is to wear one of the blue eye beads you will see in souvenir shops; or, if you think you might be about to get it, spit or make a noise similar to that of spitting. It can be a little disconcerting when, after you have admired someone's baby, they promptly expectorate.

The test to see if you have it is to try and recite at speed a piece of religious text, such as The Lord's Prayer. If you can't complete it or get muddled then you have got the evil eye and must go to one of the ladies who sit outside larger churches and she will remove it for you.

Religion

The Greek Orthodox faith is predominant everywhere in Greece although some islands have a proportion of Catholics. Orthodoxism is a splinter of the Catholic religion and has no connection with the Pope.

Services have a very relaxed atmosphere and no hymns or prayers are sung by the congregation. The faith seems to be strong and not as restrictive as some other forms of Christianity. Priests up to a certain "rank" are allowed to be married.

Churches and name days

The islands have literally hundreds of churches ranging from the very grand to those no bigger than the average garden shed! Every

This Byzantine church is a useful landmark in a maze-like village.

*Hora, Sikinos. The streets of the island's capital see an almost
continuous procession of mules and donkeys carrying firewood
to stock up for winter burning.*

family tries to build a church at some time, often painting the roof sky blue to bring them nearer to God. Each church is named after a saint and in the smaller ones services are held only on the corresponding saint's day, once a year.

In the monasteries and larger churches, the whole village will attend services giving a festival atmosphere. Similarly all Greek people are named after saints and while birthdays are not celebrated, name days are marked by visiting with gifts the homes of fellow celebrants. There is little variety of names and so on the designated day for the most common names, such as Yannis and Kostas, restaurants and nightspots are well attended to the point of bursting!

Easter

Easter is a good time to visit Greece as the celebrations are as enthusiastic as Christmas is in England (Christmas is a lesser festival in Greece). Good Friday is a day of mourning. On the Saturday everyone goes to church for a midnight service after which there may be a firework display and each household lights a candle and tries to carry it home still lit. If successful, this is a sign of good luck for the next year.

On Easter Sunday, the traditional meal is of roast lamb, and wine is free in restaurants and *tavernas* if you can find one open. People carry red eggs and the usual "good morning" or "good evening" is replaced by "Christ is risen" to which the reply is "truly risen".

Transport to and within Greece is generally full at this time, so if you are planning an Easter trip book well in advance.

AMORGOS

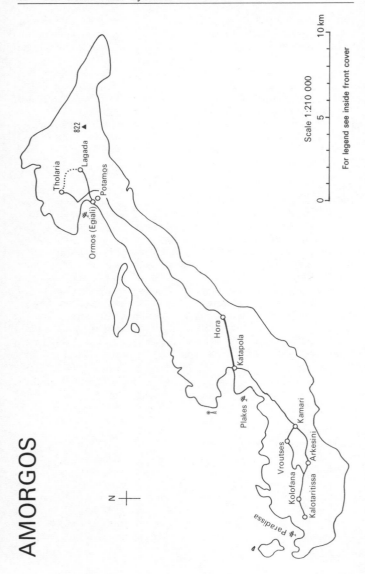

Scale 1:210 000

For legend see inside front cover

TEN

Amorgos

Population: 2,500   *Highest point: 826m*
Area: 134 sq. km.   *Hotel beds: 80*

Although the gentle island of Amorgos is very popular with its visitors, the facilities are correspondingly few. Neither is the island likely to become very commercialised as (especially in the south) water, even to drink, is scarce and this has dictated the life style of the people, who would grow more crops if only there was water for irrigation and who consequently concentrate on livestock farming and fishing.

The island is very mountainous and although a wide road has been cut to link the two largest towns of Egiali in the north and Hora in the south, it is of a poor surface and prevents them being joined by bus routes. In reasonable weather, caiques make the twenty-kilometre trip along the coast but the Cyclades has its fair share of winds and this area is worse than most, which means effectively that Amorgos can best be considered in two halves.

This island has many charming villages and attractive scenery but very few beaches. Its appeal seems to lie in its tranquillity and the unequalled friendliness of the islanders that keeps visitors returning year after year.

Arrival by sea

At the time of writing, all ferries call at both **Egiali** (Ormos) in the north and **Katapola** in the south, with fares from the mainland and other islands being the same to both ports. It is a good idea to remember the name of the port you intend to disembark at rather than relying on the name of the island, as this isn't always used in the on-board announcements and some unfortunates have been left trying to identify the "island of Egiali" while the ferry leaves from their intended destination with them still aboard.

Tickets can be purchased in both ports from conspicuous travel agents but not elsewhere. Amorgos is subject to frequent changes in timetable and itinerary as, basically, the ferry companies don't really want to go there because there is little traffic and two dockings are entailed. For the most reliable information regarding departures, ask at the port police office in Katapola; tel. 71259 or call at their office in the far right-hand street leading up from the square in the port (standing with your back to the sea).

The journey time between the island's two ports is about an hour. In summer there are at least four departures for the mainland per week, falling to two in winter or as weather permits. The vessels serving this route vary greatly in age and speed so the journey time from Piraeus can take anything from eleven to sixteen hours and is further dependent on which other islands are to be visited en route. Routes are:

- Piraeus, Paros, Amorgos.
- Piraeus, Syros, Paros, Ios, Naxos, Koufonissia, Donoussa, Amorgos.
- Amorgos, Astipalea, Nissiros, Tilos, Symi, Rhodes, Kos, Kalymnos, Leros, Lipsi, Patmos, Ikaria, Samos, Chios, Mytilini, Lemnos, Kavala.
- Amorgos, Koufonissia, Schinoussa, Iraklia, Naxos, Paros.

The last route is served by a small passenger ferry that can carry only one vehicle, and at the islands of Paros and Naxos it calls at secondary ports, entailing a bus or taxi ride for those wishing to continue on to the main towns. This vessel does have the advantage of a shallow draft which enables it to dock without the need to transfer passengers to caiques, required by larger ferries at Schinoussa, Iraklia and Koufonissia.

Road system

The road between Katapola and Hora (Amorgos town) is asphalt but elsewhere all routes are wide dirt tracks. As previously stated, the main towns are linked by a road of poor standard which is best tackled only by lorry or motorbikes of "Enduro" standard and certainly not by the mopeds commonly provided by the rent-a-bike companies.

A secluded beach seen from the road to Lagada, Amorgos.

The road from Hora to Arkesini should not be attempted in high winds since in places it is very exposed as it climbs various peaks; the possibility of being blown off the edge to land some hundred feet further down is a genuine risk. The sign post one kilometre out of Hora that reads "Kato Meria" is for Arkesini and villages beyond.

Buses In the north there are routes from Egiali, or Ormos as it is written on the timetables, to Lagada and Tholaria:

Ormos	Lagada		Ormos	Tholaria
06.40	07.00		07.10	07.20
11.30	11.45		11.00	11.15
16.00	16.15		15.30	15.45
18.00	18.15		17.30	17.45
21.30	21.45		22.00	22.30

In the south there are hourly buses from Hora to Katapola and one other route that leaves Hora to call at Aghia Anna, the Monastery, Kamari, Vroutses, Arkesini, Kolofana and Kalotaritissa. The latter has only one departure per day and so unless you plan to stay overnight at any of the stops, you must walk or hitch back. This service is run to bring the school children to Hora.

Taxi There is one taxi in the south, tel. 71255.

Petrol The rent-a-bike agent may sell you a little from his workshop on the harbour in Katapola but then again he may not!

Maps There are three maps of the island, one of the two colour versions has some information about Amorgos, Iraklia, Schinoussa, Koufonissia, Keros and Donoussa printed on the reverse side. The one with "funky" lettering on the front cover gives details of the mineral content of the various regions. The third is black and white and I saw it displayed outside "Amorgos Paris" in Ormos but had no luck finding this shop open to buy one. All three contain errors and not one shows the cross roads leading out of Ormos where the four roads go to (clockwise) Ormos, Lagada, Tholaria and the north. See our map on page 62 for details.

Accommodation

North Ormos has three hotels of which Mike is the largest and is located just above the end of the jetty. The remaining two are situated behind the beach, two hundred metres from the port. There are also rooms to rent in Ormos but very few; try following the road that ascends to the right of the jetty (back to the sea) and as it curves left and then right after the new clinic, you'll see new buildings ahead which are rooms to rent establishments — but the owner usually meets the ferries.

In Tholaria all the tavernas and cafés have rooms to rent, as does the baker. There are a few rooms available in Lagada but none in Potamos.

Hotels	Category	Tel.	Beds
Mike	C	71252	38
Lahee	D	-	30
Askas	D	-	12

South Katapola has two hotels, the Hotel Minoa on the square in the port and Kato Akrotiri concealed at the end of the little beach to the left of the jetty facing the sea.

Unlike Katapola, Hora has many rooms to rent but there are no hotels. To locate a room, the best bet is to park your bags in the café where they usually know who has vacancies, and if you don't have any luck there, set out and ask at the many houses displaying signs. There are no rooms in Arkesini but above the taverna in Kolofana there are four beds. But be sure to enquire whether there is any water.

Camping There is a rudimentary camp site behind the main beach at Katapola.

Where to eat

North In Ormos all the eating places are clustered together along the stepped path to the right of hotel Mike, with the exception of one restaurant opposite to the "telephone shop" on the street parallel to the sea front, where some very intriguing pictures are displayed. They are the sort of thing that would be well received if hung on a dentist's ceiling, as you can look at them for hours and still spot something you hadn't noticed before.

Tholaria has the Panorama, the Turquoise Taverna and two café/taverna/mini markets.

Lagada has two tavernas, one in the square and other in the side street to the left facing down hill. Potamos has no eating places whatsoever.

South Hora has six tavernas, two cafés and an Austrian owned pastry shop that sells herbal teas and stronger drinks.

Katapola's sea front road is edged with tavernas and restaurants with only the odd café and grocer's to interrupt them. On the side of the bay opposite to the jetty is a small taverna where locally caught fish are prepared to order.

Night life

Katapola has one discotheque on the far side of the port and two bars near the jetty.

What to see and do

Stroumvos
Half a kilometre north of Lagada is the remains of an abandoned village. Within this mini ghost town, some enterprising foreigners have refurbished two of the houses for summer use.

Roman tombs
Along the shore line in the port are the ruins of vaulted Roman tombs. Unfortunately I can't comment further on them as I believed the legend on the back of one of the maps which stated that the site is at Katapola and couldn't understand why no one knew anything about them when I reached the southern part of the island.

The monastery of Panayia Khozoviotissa
This is definitely worth a visit. Even if monasteries aren't usually your cup of tea, the sight of the gleaming white building clinging to the orange hillside can't fail to move you.

Take the signposted route from Hora and after three and a half kilometres, the dirt road ends and the first of many terraced steps begin. At the start you descend while rounding a rock face to approach the gates. It is at this point that the monastery first becomes visible and while you are still awestruck by the sight, your eye may be caught by the highly sophisticated sign to the left of the gate. Below an illustration of the view ahead of you are printed, in Greek and English, the conditions to be met by those wishing to enter the grounds. The notice advises you that the wearing of shorts is not permitted and that women will not be admitted unless they wear a skirt or dress of a reasonable length and have their arms covered. It also advises that clothing is not lent by the monks. I was rather taken aback by this as I had donned my most conservative outfit — a long-sleeved jump suit — but decided I would ask at the door if my attire was modest enough and hoped not to pass any monks as I ascended the long, steep stairway. Twenty minutes later and extremely out of breath, I approached the door and there wasted ten minutes being humble to a bearded man in black who turned out not to be a monk at all!

Through the narrow doorway I ascended an almost sheer staircase after donning an extremely ancient creation in the form of a button-up-the-front dress I had selected from an uninspiring collection hung just behind the door. The monk who greeted me

The Monastery of Panayia Khozoviotissa.

must have had great self-control as he didn't laugh at my appearance. We talked for a while and I was given a very detailed hand-out to read while he went to prepare a tray containing a small glass of lemon liquor from Naxos, a glass of water and some rather good Turkish delight. After patiently answering my questions he indicated that it was time to show me the church. Another three impossible staircases later we arrived at the uppermost level where a tiny church is located. I was shown the famous icon which hangs to the right of the cross and on the adjacent wall. It has been so richly overlaid with precious metals that very little of the original icon is visible. Whichever of the two stories regarding the icon's arrival in Amorgos you choose to believe, it was this artefact that caused the construction of the amazing edifice. The version favoured by the monk who was my guide tells that a group of monks were forced to flee from their monastery of Khozeva in Palestine by the iconoclastic persecution; carrying the precious icon with them, they journeyed in search of a site on which to build a new monastery. On reaching Amorgos they saw a rock face which so resembled the setting they had been forced to abandon that they took it to be a sign that they had finally found the right place to begin work.

The second and much more romantic version tells of a religious woman, a resident of Khovoza in Palestine, who in order to prevent its destruction at the hands of the iconoclasts, cast the icon adrift in a small boat. The people of Amorgos spotted this boat and built the monastery above the place where it came to rest.

The origins of the monastery are the subject of further legend that relates how each morning, on arriving at the construction site, the workers would find the previous day's work mysteriously destroyed. They were baffled until one morning they also found embedded in the cliff face, one of the long thin lengths of metal used to refine the surface of the outer walls, and hanging from it was a bag of tools. This was taken to mean that they were intended to build in this location rather than where they had begun; and so work was recommenced under the iron that remained in place until it was found on the monastery balcony in the early 1950s. It is now kept in a glass case within the monastery's church.

It was a great surprise to learn that the monastery is so narrow — only four metres at its widest point — as this is by no means obvious when viewed from below. There are some sixty rooms including accommodation for ten monks, but only four now live there and I am told that when they go to that "Greater Monastery in the Sky" the building will be closed, which would be a tragedy.

Unlike other establishments, its inhabitants have no creature comforts and although there is a telephone, electricity has not been installed. The life style of the monks revolves mainly around prayer and housework, but they also have in their care many ancient manuscripts that require repair and preservation.

Museum

Hora has a new museum on the main street just by the middle square and identifiable by a brown double doorway. I think it is fairly safe to comment on the colour of the door as it had just been painted, and so is likely to aid identification for some time to come. Open from 09.00 to 14.00 Mondays to Fridays.

The Kastro

This highly conspicuous building perches on top of a rock in the north of Hora. An exposed stairway leads up to a locked gate but the key, and probably an escort, can be obtained from Manolis Despotides or Yinakos Simos by asking at any of the shops for their present whereabouts.

Useful information

North

The telephone office is inside the tiny grocer's shop opposite the taverna that runs parallel to the sea front road. The meter isn't visible from inside the claustrophobic booth but you should be able to communicate in sign language that you want them to cut you off when the meter reaches a certain figure. The shop doesn't seem to close for siestas and stays open very late seven days a week.

Money matters Cash and cheques can be exchanged at the hotels and at the "Village Shop" in Lagada.

Stamps The shops that sell cards also sell stamps.

Health matters The island as a whole has three doctors but there doesn't seem to be much co-ordination in their leave taking and during my recent stay only one doctor still remained on the island. In Ormos, take the road up past Hotel Mike and follow it left where, after fifty metres, the new surgery sits on a corner.

There is no **pharmacy** in the north but the postman makes the journey every Monday, Wednesday and Friday to Hora and will collect the filled prescriptions for you. Ask the doctor to arrange this for you.

South

The telephone office is the last building at the bottom of the lowest square in Hora. Open from 07.30 to 15.10 Monday to Friday. Outside of these hours, the taverna next door but one has a metered phone. Unfortunately, it also has two very boisterous youngsters and trying to hear a conversation over anything but a perfect line isn't really practical. There is an international phone box opposite the post office.

Money matters The Agricultural Bank of Greece has a branch in Hora, but for tourists this is totally irrelevant as they won't perform any of the usual exchange services and refer you curtly to the post office on the adjacent corner of the square.

The post office in Hora is in a small square with the bank and international telephone kiosk, towards the top end of town. Open from 07.30 to 14.30 Monday to Friday.

Health matters The doctors' surgery in Hora is near the bakery at the lower end of town. Tel. 71207. In Arkesini the surgery is the building in front of the school. Tel. 71252.

Centres of population

Hora

The more usual route to Hora (Amorgos town) via the winding road leading up from Katapola brings a view of the entire town capping a moderate hill and dominated by the ancient Kastro, which looms over the settlement from a sheer rocky peak.

From the bakery at the lower end through to the helicopter pad at the upper end of the town runs the market street with its many tiny grocery shops, cafeniöns, tavernas and numerous churches. Evidence of the traffic of mules and donkeys abounds and the stepped streets have small rampways to one side to aid their smooth passage. Little side streets lead where you would least expect them to — often to a dead end in a mini farmyard — and it is easy to get lost after dark as street lighting is limited to the squares.

A dirt "ring road" exists linking the *platea* where the bakery is to the summit of the town where a larger parking area is found, and where the track from the northern end of the island emerges.

Amorgos, Hora, the island's capital. The rocky crag above the town was the site of a Venetian castle.

Katapola

The southern port is divided into two small hamlets that are separated by a sandy beach, backed by a camping ground and some guest houses. The cluster of buildings farthest from the dock comprises many guest houses and a few tavernas, while all the shops, the hotel and pharmacies are grouped near the jetty and the waterfront provides a setting for many bars and restaurants.

Egiali

Ormos — as the locals prefer to call what the maps show as Egiali — is a small village, but the fact that it merges into Potamos further up hill makes it look deceptively larger than it is.

On the sea front are collected all the commercial buildings: tavernas, shops, ticket offices, cafés, the telephone office and the largest hotel. Behind this area are the houses and bakery.

The port has a long sandy beach backed by a few trees and some buildings that include two hotels. The road that separates them leads on to Tholaria. The exit road from the port area passes between the donkey station and a ticket office where, after 500m, it branches to Lagada, Tholaria and the track to the south.

Lagada

This is a sleepy little village full of charm in its tiny streets and squares. Because of the lack of facilities it is more suited as a place to visit rather than to stay, and this adds to its attraction. There are a few expatriates living permanently in the community and the Englishwoman at "The Village Shop" can be called upon to help with any difficulties.

As you enter Lagada, you pass a wooded hillside and an area where the rock is studded with white wooden crosses. The lower end of the village is exceptionally green and refreshingly cool.

Amorgos, Lagada.

Tholaria

Another small, pretty village but with more tavernas and certainly more available accommodation than Lagada. Each taverna seems to double as a mini market with at least a few packets of washing powder on sale and all have rooms above for rent.

The roof tops and terraced steps that make up the main street have been painted with white flower patterns and every now and then two intertwining hearts adorn the route.

Potamos

The smallest village of the four in the north of the island, it straggles a path of steps that provide an ample source of manure for the priest to collect at sun down, since the only mode of transport is by donkey and in places multiple parking makes it difficult to edge your way around these patient animals! Potamos has nothing in the way of commercial or aesthetic interest.

Kamari

Even to call it a village is an exaggeration as the few houses and taverna that faces them from the other side of a small valley form such a small cluster that it is possible to drive past almost without noticing.

Vroutses

No sooner have you left Kamari than you come to Vroutses, and apart from the fact that there is one café in addition to the taverna, there isn't much to differentiate the two.

Arkesini

Fifteen kilometres from Hora is another assortment of buildings with very little appeal. It has one café and a doctors surgery but nothing else worth noting. Some of the locals told me that they would very much like to enter the tourist industry but there is such a severe shortage of water even for themselves, that a taverna — let alone a hotel — is out of the question.

Kolofana and Kalotaritissa

Three and four kilometres from Arkesini respectively, the latter has two rooms above a taverna and I can only hope that the owner struck lucky when choosing a site to sink a well. Kalotaritissa is the nearest settlement to the much sign posted Paradissa beach.

Beaches

In both **Ehiali** and **Katapola,** the beaches are sandy, long, narrow and attractive. In the north, the road that leads up to **Tholaria** passes two more isolated and wider beaches, the latter being where most nudists gather.

In the south, **Plakes** beach, two kilometres north along the coast from Katapola, can only be reached on foot. **Paradissa** beach just before Kalotaritissa is a pleasant but small sandy stretch.

Historical background

Evidence of habitation on Amorgos can be traced back as far as 3300BC from the many excavations that have been made and some of the artefacts are now on display in Oxford and Sweden. The three main settlements were all near the present day sites of Egiali, Katapola and Arkesini which were colonised by the Militians, Samians and Naxians respectively; each community minted its own coinage from silver.

In 322BC the last major Greek naval battle took place off the island's shores where the Athenians were defeated by the Macedonians. The rule of Amorgos was held by the Dukes of Naxos and the Quirinis of Astipalea at intervals throughout the Latin period except when in 1267 it fell into Greek hands again for a short while.

The islanders were forced to flee to Naxos for safety when the constant attacks by pirates, to which they were particularly vulnerable because of the island's isolation, became too much to bear.

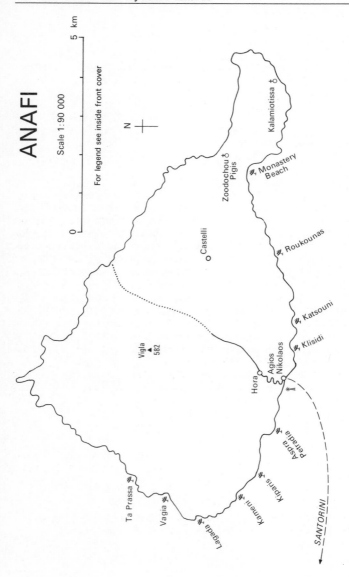

ANAFI

Scale 1:90 000

For legend see inside front cover

N

Zoodochou Pigis

Kalamiotissa

Monastery Beach

Castelli

Roukounas

Katsouni

Klisidi

Vigla 582

Hora

Agios Nikolaos

Aspra Petradia

Kiparis

Kameni

Lagada

Vagia

Ta Prassa

SANTORINI

ELEVEN

Anafi

Population: 350   *Highest point: data unavailable*
Area: 38 sq. km.   *Beds: 55*

Anafi, a sandy coloured island with occasional vivid green valleys between its gently curving hills and mountains, is not only new to tourism, it is also new to what we might think of as civilisation. Every house now has electricity but this was only supplied within the last twelve years. Telephones have recently been converted from the "wind the handle" type and the island has only one video.

While more visitors arrive each year, Anafi has made few changes to cater for them. The islanders are very unworldly but much written about, and an eminent social anthropologist has made studies there for twenty year of the traditional way of life in an isolated community and of the effects of tourism on it.

High on top of the mountain above the port is Hora, the island's only village, an attractive but unspectacular settlement that takes about three hours to explore thoroughly at a leisurely pace. In contrast to Santorini, only two hours away by ferry, the island's many beaches are of golden sand and edged by trees.

Arrival by sea

Four times a week a large passenger and car ferry calls at **Agios Nikolaos,** the port of Anafi, as it makes a circular tour of the area. The exact route varies according to how many other ferries are in service and which islands they call at. Routes are:
- Piraeus, Santorini, Anafi.
- Piraeus, Milos, Folegandros, Santorini, Anafi.
- Anafi, Crete (Agios Nikolaos and Sitea), Kassos, Karpathos and Rhodes

Apart from the above, there is also a weekly caique from Santorini that arrives mid-morning on Wednesdays and returns immediately after unloading. Passengers are carried for the same price as the ferry. None of the travel offices on Santorini seemed to know anything about this alternative so I suggest you enquire at the port police office in Fira. Tel. 22239. In high season there are twice weekly day trips from Santorini and it is sometimes possible to arrange with the captain to let you stay over and make a delayed return. He does, however, need to know in advance of your intended date of return and so firm arrangements must be made.

Tickets can be bought in the little port from the office inside a converted boat shed. They open two hours before each departure. The island has no port police and so one of the two regular policemen performs these duties.

Road system

There isn't one! Obviously, there is a route from the port to the village but even the locals think twice about the ascent that takes an hour on foot. Donkeys are difficult to track down and I wouldn't want to be a passenger on one of the island's five or six motorbikes. There are no four-wheel vehicles and no petrol can be obtained. It is illegal to take petrol aboard the ferries except inside the fuel tank of vehicles and so you must use your imagination to work out what is in those heavy boxes the locals bring with them.

The track from the port is stepped for the first 200m but small ramps of cement have been placed at random to enable the bikes to slalem up and down! Where the concrete ends the track becomes surfaced with loose stones among rocky bumps and dips until after 800m it reconverts to cement again for the last 500m.

The ascent is very steep and corners are extremely tight. Efficient brakes and nerves of steel are essential for the descent. I had the first but not the second of these qualities and because I have got short legs I couldn't steady the bike while the front wheel was on a lower step than the back wheel. Also being rather short in the trunk (no sympathy please) I couldn't see the position of the next ramp in time to aim for it; so when I finally reached terra firma, I felt the need of a very stiff drink.

The track begins behind the electricity generating station and to the left.

Accommodation

There are no hotels or guesthouses on Anafi, only rooms. In summer, those Anafians who have left and gone to live in Athens return to escape the heat and fill many of the available beds. There are only eight double rooms in the port and no more than twenty-five in the village with a further three above Klisidi beach.

If you aren't prepared to join the many others camping on the beaches then it's best to find someone who speaks Greek, such as a travel agent, to telephone ahead and reserve a room for you if any are available. The geography of the village, lack of landmarks and the fact that no "rooms for rent" signs appear, make it impossible for me to describe to you the whereabouts of the owners and their phone numbers:

Yiannis Sigalas	61237	8 beds, own bath
Margarita Kaloyeropoulou	61235	6 beds
Yiakovos Rousous	61238	2 bed apartment
Vikendios Gavala	61234	6 beds
Ireni Damivou	61204	8 beds
Kiriakos Andoniaris	61202	4 beds (not recommended)
Lefteria Kolida	no phone	2 beds
Powpi Rousou	61218	15 beds (port area)
Marie Garcionaria	61268	2 beds (port area)

Camping is tolerated but fires are illegal. On the beaches, as elsewhere, rainwater is collected and stored in concrete tanks. Unfortunately there have been cases of visitors thoughtlessly washing their clothes or hair with this precious water and the whole year's supply has been contaminated.

If you don't like the idea of washing in the sea, bear in mind that, because of the shortage of drinkable water, what comes out of the tap will be from a well and extremely brackish. Having finally worked up a lather in your hands to try and wash your face, as soon as you apply more water to rinse, it seems to set and you end up feeling more oily than before you started! I can't imagine what it is like to wash your hair in it but as long as you use the local detergent, it is possible to do the odd bit of laundry.

Where to eat

There is one restaurant in the village but it has a rather limited selection of food. Two others in the port and one above Klisidi beach make up the list.

At the end of the season all supplies are run down and choice can be very small. Fruit and vegetables are rare on the island as they are largely brought from the mainland. Meat isn't in great abundance but things have improved since refrigerators were introduced and many of the locals are fishermen whose catches compare very favourably in price to those on larger islands.

Night life

There is one bar in the port: The Crazy Shrimp, and three cafés in the village, none of which are likely to wear you out.

What to see and do

Castelli
This is the site of the island's original settlement. It's very much in ruins, especially since thieves carted off the detachable heads of the statues and possibly other treasures that were awaiting excavation in the area too. New digging was discovered at the same time as the heads were reported stolen and, as there had been a yacht moored off the coast at that point, it will probably never be known what else was removed. There is now someone employed to check on this area and that of the monastery to prevent a recurrence.

Zoodohou Pigis Monastery
The monastery can be visited when demand is sufficient as caiques leave the port to make the 40-minute journey along the southern coast. Having passed the island's best beaches the boats leave you at the tiny jetty where the path begins for the short and not too taxing climb to the monastery.

The earthquake of 1956 badly damaged both the church and the monks cells that surround it to form a small courtyard within the rectangle. Renovation has been enthusiastically undertaken and this has left it looking more modern than the buildings in the village except for one small building with an arched doorway that is used as a store room for the ladders.

There is one priest living there, a young fellow who hastily donned his robes over gum boots and workmen's clothes, as he had been helping the family from the neighbouring house to mix cement. He was distinctly unfriendly even though I was respectful in both behaviour and dress.

Anafi. The route up to the almost inaccessible temple seen from the grounds of the Zoodohos Pigis Monastery.

Kalamiotissa Monastery

Between the house and monastery wall is a sign pointing to the Kalamiotissa Monastery 1.5kms away. This looks more encouraging than it should for when you turn the corner and look in the direction indicated, no path is visible to the dome of the church that lies behind a very high mountain. A donkey and guide would be essential for the oneway, one and a half hour journey.

The caique costs 1,250 for the single trip. I arranged to be picked up one hour later which was ample but there is an excellent beach there that you may want to spend some time at.

Useful information

The post office in Hora is fortunately well signposted as, apart from normal postal services, it houses the telephone "office" and is the only place to change money. Cash, travellers cheques and Eurocheques present no problem but those who have put money into a Greek bank account won't be able to get any out on Anafi.

The only employee, Manolis, is very helpful but speaks little English. Opening hours are 08.00 to 15.00, Monday to Friday.

If you need to make a **telephone** call outside of the above hours, there are four metered phones: one in the village, one at the taverna nearest the jetty in the port, and two at Klisidi beach.

Health There is usually a "National Service" **doctor** on the island but a month may pass between one leaving and his replacement arriving. The only pharmacy is within the surgery. (If the surgery is closed, enquire at the first cafenión as you enter the Hora.) To find the surgery, descend the widest steps from the square at the far end of the village and head right. If you keep stopping to look back up, you will eventually see the sign. Tel. 61215.

Police This office is very difficult to find and it's even harder to describe its location. I was fortunate because a villager had noticed that there was a green towel hanging on the washing line so gave me a "landmark", but I don't suppose this is a permanent fixture! Ask in one of the cafés for the "astee noh mée ah"; you might find an off-duty policeman in there anyway. Tel. 612.

Centres of population

Agios Nikolaos

The port contains only eight or nine buildings and most of these are boat sheds. It is quite an attractive area once you get out of the view of the electricity generating station. On your right, with your back to the sea, is a tiny shop that opens very irregularly. The two taverna/rooms are both to the left while the bar is at the side of the track to Hora.

In the winter all the larger fishing vessels are taken to Koufonissia (a neighbouring island) as the harbour at Anafi offers no protection from bad weather.

Hora

A small and pretty enough village, Hora rambles between the school and up to the small square. The school has only seven pupils to its two teachers as many of the young people have drifted to the mainland to live and a lot of the houses are consequently empty. The emigrants don't lose touch with the island, however, as there is an active society of ex-resident Anafians who have sponsored the new community centre and equipped it with a video.

The little streets seem to have more chickens than pedestrians. Three small shops and a baker's are to be found on the widest of the streets. Olive oil, a famous honey and *kephalotiri* (a hard, strong cheese suitable for grating onto spaghetti) are exported and the islanders make a dry red wine for their own consumption.

Anafi. The sandy coastline near the monastery Zoodohos Pigis.

Beaches

Contrary to what I have seen in print about Anafi, the island has an abundance of beaches. From the port heading east after the small patch of sand in front of the boat sheds, **Klisidi** has a café and taverna above its long sandy length. This is the most popular beach and many people camp there. Next is **Katsouni** beach where nudists

The beach below Zoodohos Pigis Monastery.

are encouraged to go; then **Roukounas,** the largest beach and then **Monastery Beach.** Between those mentioned are numerous small areas of sand and trees, some having water available. The sea on this coast is never of "mill pond" stillness but neither is it up to surfing standard.

West from the port are **Aspra Petradia** with its white stones that are collected by the locals and decorated for sale, **Kiparisi, Kameni, Lagada, Vagia** and **Ta Prassa.** These are all pebble beaches and difficult to get to overland.

Once a year the locals have to undertake an unusual harvest of the toilet paper left by campers that gets blown up and caught on the branches of the trees.

Historical background

According to mythology, Anafi is the creation of Apollo who caused it to rise from the sea to provide shelter for Jason and his Argonauts who were in danger of losing both the golden fleece and their lives in a severe storm. Not surprisingly then, the ruins at Castelli and Kalamiotissa are of temples built to worship Apollo, but little remains to be seen of them today.

By Greek standards, Anafi has had very few conquerors unless the recording of its history is incomplete. The island was once given as a gift to Guglielmo Crispi by his brother Sanudo, the twelfth Duke of Naxos. Until the Turkish occupation, the island was plagued by pirate raids and the fortress built by Guglielmo afforded little protection. Troubles also came in another form as the volcanic eruptions on neighbouring Santorini sent clouds of dust that increased the mass of the island and rendered it temporarily uninhabitable.

In more recent times, political exiles from the mainland and those thought to be mad were sent to end their days on the island. These included many scholars who held lectures in order to keep their minds active. Some were artists and their work can still be seen in the form of murals in some of the village houses.

FOLEGANDROS

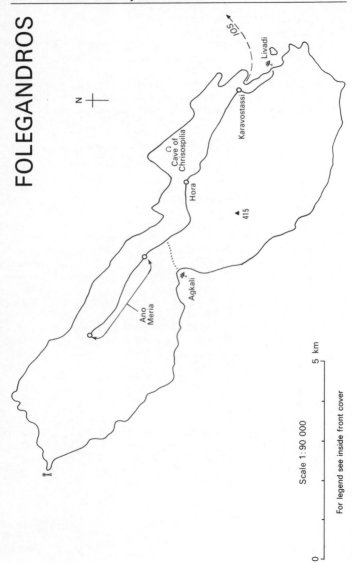

Scale 1:90 000

For legend see inside front cover

0   5 km

TWELVE

Folegandros

Population: 750	*Highest point: 445m*
Area: 32 sq. km.	*Hotel beds: 110*

Like Santorini, Folegandros is high, narrow and extremely rocky; indeed its name is taken from the Pheonician word meaning little rock. Unlike Santorini however, its colouring is of pastels — light grey, beige and yellows — and its surface undulates into many mountains and hills. The port is situated at the base of its one gentle incline and the two villages are set high on inland peaks.

A comparatively uncommercialised island, Folegandros is completely lacking in souvenir shops and tourist-style eating places, but there is much construction in progress of buildings large enough to suggest that they will be hotels and pensions. The changes will come soon enough. In the meantime Folegandros is the ideal place to enjoy getting away from it all. If you aren't too bothered about sandy beaches, museums, archaeological sites and monasteries, then the island has just enough tavernas, cafés and bars to encourage a family feeling amongst its visitors.

Arrival by sea

Only the large car and passenger ferries call at **Karavostassi,** the port of Folegandros. There are daily departures in summer, dwindling to twice a week in winter. Routes are:

- Piraeus, Paros, Naxos, Ios, Sikinos, Folegandros.
- Piraeus, Milos, Folegandros.
- Folegandros, Santorini, Anafi.

There are two ticket offices in Hora and one in Ano Meria but their

Folegandros. One of the old houses in Kastro. Barricades constructed between it and its neighbour were at least a temporary deterrent to would-be raiders.

opening hours are irregular so perhaps the best bet is to buy them in the cement shed at the start of the jetty. Most of the locals are well informed about the schedules.

Road system

The road from the port, Karavostassi, into Hora and onto Ano Meria is of cement and, apart from one or two pot holes, the surface is good.

As far as Hora it is possible to pull off to the side of the road in order to let another vehicle pass; however, between Hora and Ano Meria the narrow road is sided by stone walls and, although passing points have been built into the route, they are few and far between. The bus hoots like mad when it nears bends and hill tops, which is a very sensible idea.

As you near Hora from either direction, there are "no-entry" signs posted but everybody seems to ignore them and, as there is no alternative route to complete the second half of the journey, it is necessary to go into the village.

Buses The island has only two buses; you enter at the front and pay before you get off. The driver does not get a fixed wage but lives on the money collected from fares so the locals often tell him to keep the change. Departure times are:
- Hora to the port: 7.20, 2.30, 5.00.
  Also one hour before ferry departures.
  Ten minutes journey time, immediate return. The bus leaves from outside the school in the war memorial square.
- Hora to Ano Meria: 8.00, 1.30, 3.00 and 7.00. Wait by the sign post to the *Ouzeria* at the bottom of the slope down from Hotel Fani Vevis.
- Ano Meria to Hora: 7.00, 2.00 and 5.00.
  Journey time 30 minutes. Maximum fare 120 drs.

If you want to get on the bus other than at one of its starting points then you must wait at one of the cement huts as at other places the road is so steep that the bus can't stop its five kilometre an hour crawl to let you in!

Taxis There aren't any.

Vehicle hire There isn't any.

Petrol Guess what? That's right, there isn't any! The locals have their own barrels which are replaced with full ones by a boat that also brings gas canisters. Fill up before you go.

Maps An adequate map with very little information printed on the back is available at the ticket office in the Kastro. In the port, on the wall near the concrete shelter, is a linen hand-painted map with information pinned to it. Useful for initial orientation although some of the figures are rather deceptive and Ano Meria reads like a budding tourist resort.

Accommodation

Beds aren't difficult to find but few places have their own bathroom or hot water. I recommend negotiations with the people who meet the boat.

Hotel	Telephone	No. of beds	Location
Hotel Yiorgis	41205	22	(port area)
Hotel Odyseus	41239	12	(Hora)
Hotel Danasi	41230	27	(Hora)
Hotel Fani Vevis	41237	49	(Hora)
Rooms			
Maria Yeradou	41265	12	(Hora)
Irene Sideri	41235	20	(Hora)
Pavlos Sideri	41205	10	(port area)

The only camping ground is to the left of the port (with your back to the sea). Past the Hotel Yiorgis the road becomes sand for a while and then resumes as a dirt track leading over the hill and down onto a small sandy beach. There are the usual facilities but no phone. A torch is essential if you have to make the journey after dark.

Apart from the official site, there is nowhere flat enough to pitch a tent!

Where to eat

In the port there are three taverna/cafés and one bar. Hora has one snack bar, one pizza place, two cafés, two restaurants and two bars. The restaurant opposite the butcher's shop (same owner) serves the best barbecued chicken I have ever tasted!

Nightlife

There are two well signposted bars in Hora; one describes itself as a "music bar". Visitors usually congregate at the restaurant and stay on long after their food is finished.

What to see and do

Museum The powers that be are at the moment looking for a suitable building to rent and use to display whatever it is that they now have in a store room. As the island has no archaeological sites, it's difficult to imagine what will be on exhibition.

Golden Cave They tell me that this cave is full of stalactites and bones (see Historical background) but as they also tell me it needs rope, crampons and extreme courage to get to, I didn't go! Good luck. A film crew with suitable equipment made the descent a few years ago and found that there was insufficient oxygen in places!

Folegandros. The main street in Kastro, "The Village Within the Walls."

Useful information

Post office Open from 08.00—14.30 Monday to Friday, this is also the telephone office. From the main square in Hora, pass both restaurants and it is straight ahead and highly conspicuous.

Other telephones There are six metered phones on the island. In Hora when the post office is closed, a small room with an unofficial sign outside saying "O.T.E. and Telephone" will be open until 23.00. It is signposted from the main square and near the bakers. In the port, a tiny building with a long menu outside, at the start of the ascent to Hora, acts as a telephone office. The dialling code for Folegandros is 0286.

Police Inside the Kastro at the entrance nearest the baker's is the "police station", identifiable only by a very inconspicuous flag pole outside. When I went, there was nobody there.

Health matters Stand with your back to the post office, take the first turning right and continue until you come to a sign on the left that reads "Ships Tickets"; turn left there and fifty metres down on the right is the surgery/pharmacy, open 09.00—13.30 and 18.00—19.00, not Wednesdays.

Banks There aren't any. Exchange at the ticket office in Kastro or at the Post Office.

Centres of population

Hora

The island's main settlement is an extremely pleasant and compact village. As you arrive from the port, a small square provides parking beside the war memorial and bougainvillia decked school. Behind the memorial, a dazzlingly white wall marks the road leading up to the large church of Panayia (unfortunately locked) where an excellent view of the village and larger parts of the island can be enjoyed.

In the opposite direction the street leads to a larger square where tables from the *cafenion* on the corner are shaded by a small cluster of trees. To the right is the entrance to Kastro, where the little streets are lined by two-storey buildings closely packed together; by closing the gaps between them with heavy doors, the villagers provided themselves with some protection from raiding pirates in years gone by. Inside the Kastro are the Hotel Danasi, bakery, police station, ticket office, a small shop and just under a dozen rooms for rent. The exit from Kastro is onto the same square at the point where two side streets leave, later to merge at the water fountain. To the right, facing the fountain, are the two restaurants, Post Office, and the dirt track to Hotel Odyseus. To the left is the entrance to the street where you find the signposted turning to the music bar, and it leads to the bus stop (used by those going to Ano Meria) and on to the Hotel Fani Vevis, where the village ends.

Ano Meria

The name means "upper part" and it is situated along the top of a long hilly range where its various buildings straggle for some three kilometres. Here there are very few rooms to rent — and indeed most people would surely prefer to stay in Hora, although it is worth taking the time to visit Ano Meria.

The port

The port has been given a very apt name, as Karavostassi means "ship-stop"! The houses are mostly summer residences for the locals and mainlanders and, apart from these, there is very little to be found in the area. The road from the jetty forks to the left to the Hotel Yiorgis, a few heavily signposted apartments for rent and then on to the camping ground at Livadi beach. To the right are the telephone "office", eating places, bar, some rooms for rent and the road to Hora.

Beaches

I was provided with the names of at least 10 beaches, although it was pointed out to me that they were small and stony, so the word "beach" was not at all appropriate. The island is high and steep where the land and sea meet so that even where a small amount of sand or pebbles have managed to accumulate, the cliff above can be so sheer that you can only reach it by caique;

At the port is a pebbly tree-lined beach and beyond the headland is **Livadi,** where the beach is slightly more well endowed with sand and trees. A third beach, **Agkali,** is situated half way between Hora and Ano Meria but the path down to it is daunting with very little attraction at the bottom.

Folegandros. The port Karavostassis which aptly enough means "Boat stop"

Historical background

The island's first colonists were Cares who were later joined by
Phoenicians, Cretans and Dores. Both in Roman times and during
the rule of the Junta, the island was used as a refuge by exiles.

Little of the island's history is chronicled and it has remained
unmentioned in mythology but the islanders tell a dramatic story of
an event said to have taken place during the Turkish occupation.
When the villagers saw the approach of enemy ships, it was decided
to abandon their homes and seek safety in the cave of Chrisospilia.
One old woman was delayed in her flight and, when caught by the
attackers, was promised her life in return for knowledge of the
whereabouts of the hiding place. She told them, and was promptly
dispatched over the edge of a cliff. Fires were lit at the entrance to
the cave to persuade the occupants to come out but they remained
inside and suffocated to death. I am told that as well as numerous
stalactites the cave is still littered with bones.

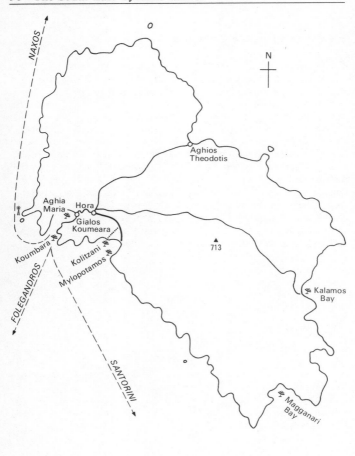

NAXOS

FOLEGANDROS

SANTORINI

N

Aghios
Theodotis

Aghia
Maria
Hora
Gialos
Koumeara
Koumbara
Kolitzani
Mylopotamos

713

Kalamos
Bay

Magganari
Bay

IOS

Scale 1:150 000

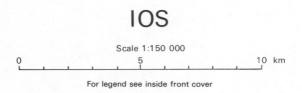

0   5   10 km

For legend see inside front cover

THIRTEEN

Ios

Population: 1,500 *Highest point: 750m*
Area: 108 sq. km. *Hotel beds: 855*

Ios, although not small by Cycladic standards, has surprisingly few settlements; apart from the port and Hora, the only developments are entirely for the benefit of tourists and situated at two of the island's best beaches. While Ios has the usual mountainous regions, they are not barren rock as with some of its neighbours and some degree of cultivation would surely be possible were it not for a chronic water shortage that plagues the island. This problem may actually come to the attention of the visitors — whose usual aim is to drink anything *but* water — if only when nothing comes out of their taps. Bottled water is sold but it makes for an expensive way to take a shower and, in the peak months, even these supplies have been known to run out. The tourist habit of taking at least one shower per day, if only to wash off the deposits of salt that the Aegean leaves on the skin, together with the "anything goes" attitude of some revellers, has led to disharmony between tourists and locals; but as this once fishing-orientated island now depends largely on tourism for its economic survival, visitors are tolerated.

In the sixties the flower children headed for Ios but they have long since been superseded by those who have heard that Ios is the "Party Island" with Tequila Slammers at from 100 drachmas a shot. Further attractions are the long sandy beaches that provide an ideal setting for sleeping off a hangover, and the fact that there aren't any archaeological sites or museums that might otherwise give you a slightly guilty conscience that none of your pursuits had so far been of the cultural variety.

Although Ios is reported to be one of the three largest hard drug centres in Greece, I found no evidence of this, but then my home island of Paros is top of the list and I haven't noticed anything there either. In summer the police force is boosted by an additional thirty men and having heard a description of how young foreign offending drunks are sobered up, I suggest, if only for this reason, that you refrain from becoming a public nuisance!

Arrival by sea

Gialos, the port of Ios, is visited by many different types of craft, including the super-fast catamarans, conventional car ferries and small, passenger-only boats. As you would expect, there are numerous travel offices including an Olympic Airways branch (although there is no airport on the island or any plans to build one). I was given misleading information in two out of three so check with more than one before consolidating your arrangements. Routes are:

- Piraeus, Syros, Paros, Naxos and Ios.
- Piraeus, Paros, Naxos, Ios.
- Ios, Naxos, Mykonos, Paros.
- Ios, Santorini.
- Ios, Sikinos, Folegandros, Santorini.
- Ios, Santorini, Crete.
- Ios, Paros, Mykonos.

The last two routes are served by the catamarans. There are also day trips to Santorini, Sikinos, Folegandros and Paros.

Road system

The route from the port, Gialos, through Hora and on to Mylopotamos is a wide asphalted road. The other routes to Aghios Theodotis and Kalamos Bay are dirt tracks and slow progress is necessary for all vehicles. This is one island that isn't best explored by bike as there are so few roads and paths to take, and both buses and caiques serve even the more remote places you may want to get to.

Buses The service from Gialos to Hora and Mylopotamos runs every 45 minutes until 23.00 hrs. Departures leave Hora from outside the police station on the main road. Additional buses operate to meet all ferry arrivals.

Ios. The island's capital and scene of all the nightly festivities, with the disused windmills looking on.

Taxis There are surprisingly few taxis to cater for those people who stay in the port and aren't ready to retire before the last bus makes the descent from Hora. Perhaps the following paragraph explains this anomaly.

Petrol There are no petrol stations anywhere on the island and the locals purchase what they need from the man who owns the piece of waste land full of oil drums, just down hill from the police station. He has placed a sign outside his front door (opposite the storage dump) that reads in English "No petrol for sale". Try the rent-a-bike offices and grovel!

Vehicle rental There isn't, and isn't likely to be, any car rental agency. Motor bikes can be rented in the port, Mylopotamos and in Hora. Be sure you have got a full tank before you set off!

Accommodation

Both hotel transit vans and housewives with a room or two to let meet the boats. It is a good idea to have decided at which centre you wish to stay and to make sure of the location of the room before you agree to go and see it.

Rooms

Behind the police station in Hora are a cluster of rooms-to-let houses. In the port many new buildings have been constructed behind the beach road and those that aren't hotels are largely rooming houses.

Camping

Ios has three camp grounds, two of which are at opposite ends of the beach at Mylopotamos. The third is to the far right of the port (facing inland) and its enormous sign is one of the first things you notice as the ferry approaches the island.

There are "African village" style bamboo huts for rent at **Kalamos Bay** and I have included them under this section because living in one must surely amount to "roughing it". The bamboo has been used so sparingly that it offers no protection from wind, rain or prying eyes.

Camping outside the official sites is not tolerated and there have been instances of an early morning passport collection from offenders, to whom the documents were returned after they had paid a stiff fine.

Hotels	Category	Tel. No.	Beds	Location
Chryssi Akti	B	91255	19	Hora
Ios	B	91224	86	Mylopotamos
Akti Iou	C	-	42	Hora
Armadoros	C	91201	50	Hora
Corali	C	91272	25	Hora
Delfini	C	91340	33	Mylopotamos
Georgos Irini	C	91527	44	Hora
Homer's Inn	C	91365	34	Hora
Mare Monte	C	91585	52	Hora
Petra	C	-	16	Hora
Phillipou	C	91290	22	Hora
Sea Breeze	C	91285	28	Gialos
Afrodite	D	91546	24	Hora
Aktaeon	D	91207	15	Hora
Leto	D	91279	71	Gialos
Mylopotamos	D	91301	44	Mylopotamos
Nissos Ios	D	91306	36	Mylopotamos
Omiros	D	91534	24	Gialos
Acropolis	E	91303	27	Hora
Aegeon	E	91392	33	Hora
Helena	E	91276	43	Hora
Markos Beach	E	91571	48	Hora
Parthenos	E	91275	19	Hora
Violetta	E	-	20	Hora

Kalamos Bay, where "African Village" style bamboo huts may be rented.

Where to eat

It is never necessary to be hungry on Ios as there are at least two twenty-four-hour take-aways selling hamburgers and toasted sandwiches. "Saini" (sigh ée nee), just around the corner from the Olympic Airways office, has fresh and well prepared food with a large number of dishes to choose from in the heated display cabinet.

Just up and to the right from the National Bank, is an arched doorway and within is a very up-market restaurant that serves some of the more unusual Greek dishes.

"Zorba's" have a delicious mushroom garnished steak. They also have free entertainment as the wooden floor moves when anyone walks near your table, at which time the wine bottle makes a dive for the floor. In places it is also necessary to organise a rota system so that one person holds the table while the others eat.

The hill side behind the police station is the setting for a very good roast-meat taverna.

Owing to the chronic water shortage that plagues Ios, much of the island is uncultivated.

Nightlife

I can't possibly list all the bars and discothèques on the island because they change too often and there are so many of them that if you can't see or hear them for yourself then you are already a stretcher case! A range of gimmicks is employed to tempt you into one particular establishment rather than any of the competitors, and everything from Greek dancing to pornographic videos is on offer. One bar has even centred its theme around calling home though the atmosphere is somewhat livelier than that found in the O.T.E. to pass the time while waiting for an international line.

Tequila Slammers are advertised at ridiculously cheap prices in all the bars. For the uninitiated, they consist of Tequila, lemonade and crème de cacao. The slammer part is both what you do with the glass on a flat surface before pouring the effervescing concoction down your throat without pause, and what happens to your head on the floor as you fall off your stool backwards after downing your fourth.

What to see and do

There are daily boat trips to Magganari Bay and further afield to Santorini, Sikinos, Folegandros and Paros. It is necessary to book seats at least one day in advance for the trips to other islands.

Plakotos, the area on the northern tip of Ios, is reported to be Homer's burial place but whatever monuments may have existed there have long since disappeared. There are also many sea caves in this region that can be explored by caique or mask and snorkel.

Water skiing and wind surfing equipment can be hired on Mylopotamos and Magganari beaches.

Useful information

Police, doctor and post office All three facilities share a large building on the main road in Hora, opposite the play ground and bus stop. Police, Tel. 91222. Doctor, Tel. 91227.

Telephone office The O.T.E. is on the corner of the first street in Hora after taking the right hand fork behind the church. Open from 07.30 to 15.00 Monday to Friday. Outside these hours, calls can be made from travel offices and The Cosmopolitan Centre. It becomes nigh on impossible to get a line outside the island, let alone an international line, very early in the season.

Money matters The National and Commercial banks both have branches in Hora.

Reading matter The book shop nearest the kiosk in the square at the port, has a reasonable selection of paperbacks and newspapers in English.

Ios. The port of Gialos seen from across the bay.

Centres of population

Gialos

The port of Ios stretches leisurely around the bay that affords the caiques and fishing boats safe harbour however much the Aegean may rage outside its refuge. The geography is such that you can't see the ferry approaching until it is almost at the jetty, where the sight of the long sandy beach and beauty of the port reassure disembarking passengers that they made a wise choice of destination.

The area behind the beach is filling up with the many hotels and boarding houses but although Gialos is the residential centre for visitors, most people opt to head for the town for their entertainment. Nevertheless, there are ample cafés and tavernas nearby and plenty of diversions along the shore line should you tire of soaking up the sun.

Hora

The island's only town is reached from the port by means of either a winding asphalted road or a stepped path, both of which have enough bars along their courses to provide adequate refreshment points. Three kilometres along the road or twenty minutes up the path bring you to where the buses stop. At first sight, especially during the day, it is hard to imagine the town throbbing to the sound of every type of music known to human ears and the little streets so full of tourists heading for their favourite bar that you sometimes get swept along with them whether that was your intended destination or not.

Opposite the post office/police station/surgery building are the playground and Evangelical church, from behind which start the two streets that form the entrances to the maze within. If you take the right hand turning it passes the O.T.E., Olympic Airways office and bakery, while the route to the left begins with the National Bank and passes innumerable discos and bars before joining the other street again.

Ios. Hora town.

Ios. The popular resort of Mylopotamos with its long golden beach.

Mylopotamos
Like the port, this long sandy beach is surrounded by all the
facilities you could wish for including two camping grounds,
restaurants, bars and nearby discotheques. Half-an-hour's walk
from Hora and served by the buses, this resort is a popular
destination with sunseekers.

Beaches

Ios is well blessed with beaches and despite the number of bodies
in search of a parking place in which to acquire a tan, it is still
possible to find a quiet spot if you put a bit of effort into it.

Kolitzani, sign-posted 500 metres before Mylopotamos and
Koumbara, ten minutes walk further along the coast past the
camping ground at Gialos, are comparatively quiet beaches and are
unofficially used by nudists.

The most popular beaches are **Mylopotamos,** the port beach and
Magganari (reached by caique) where pedaloes, wind-surfing and
water-skiing are available for those with an inclination to combine
exercising with tanning. **Aghia Maria,** two kilometres north of the
port, and **Kalamos Bay,** eight kilometres north-east along a dirt
road from Hora, both have tavernas close by.

Historical background

The history of Ios is little documented and few excavations have
been made there. In 1770 a little fame came to the island when a
Dutch traveller claimed to have discovered Homer's tomb at
Plakotos. This was never endorsed by the scholars and the supposed
site was destroyed by an earthquake in 1951, which also caused all
the water to drain from the harbour before rushing back and
destroying many buildings.

Attracted by the excellent harbour, pirates used this island as a
lair. They did encounter some resistance, however, and the gate of
Aghios Theodotis shows the hole made by the attackers that allowed
one man at a time to enter the settlement where the people were
seeking refuge. Each pirate that entered was met by a deluge of
boiling oil which successfully thwarted the attack.

KIMOLOS

Scale 1 : 90 000

0   5 km

For legend see inside front cover

FOURTEEN

Kimolos

Population: 784   *Highest point: 358m*
Area: 36 sq. km.   *Beds: 60*

The smallest of all the Cyclades islands, Kimolos remains completely uncommercialised. The landscape has fewer hills and mountains than that of its neighbours Milos and Sifnos, and the impression given by the myriad of colours belies the water shortage that exists there. The community has plans to sink three wells in the hope of finding a new source but until at least then the island will continue to depend on water brought from Athens.

Seventy per cent of the population are receiving a retirement pension. Rather than following the more typical pursuits of fishing and farming, most of the men here are sailors and, indeed, the family that owns the car ferries which serve the island are from Kimolos.

The only exports are of minerals, including components used in cement-making and kaolin for pharmaceuticals. The whole atmosphere of the island is of slow decline but surprisingly this doesn't have a depressing effect and the situation may be remedied as the younger generation no longer leave for the mainland on reaching maturity unless the choice of a sea-faring career compels it. For every two houses used as domiciles, there is one in ruins and the dark stonework crumbling by the side of newly whitewashed walls is a strange sight.

The newest building is an old people's home, a rare thing on Greek islands, and from its setting on the side of a small hill, the residents are afforded a wonderful view of the cemetery below, enabling them to contemplate things to come, in the pleasantest way possible.

The little community has an extremely grand church in the centre of the village and its red and silver domes are a useful landmark, a welcome thing in this maze-like settlement.

Arrival by sea

Psathi, the port of Kimolos, is a port of call for ferries serving only one route but the itinerary is extended once a week to include a stop at Syros, where other routes may be joined to provide an alternative to going back to Piraeus. Routes are:

● Piraeus, Kythnos, Serifos, Sifnos and Kimolos.
● Kimolos to Milos
● Kimolos, Milos and Syros.

These routes are used by two ferries: one is the standard car ferry and the other a much smaller vessel that can accommodate about twenty vehicles. In addition to these, a small converted fishing boat connects Kimolos with the secondary port of Pollonia on Milos. Departure times are 06.30 and 13.30 daily, weather permitting. This boat can squeeze on two motorbikes which then have to be held upright by their owners.

There are two fishing boats that regularly spend a few days moored in Psathi, before leaving to call at Anafi and Antiparos. They may be willing to give you a lift if you can communicate with them but you must take provisions for the trip.

Tickets are theoretically available from an agent that arrives to meet each ship; the reality however is that he will tell you to buy them on board, which proves to be twenty per cent cheaper. The two shipping lines covering the island have agencies in different grocers' shops in the village, who were willing to give me the information I needed but not to sell me a ticket. There is a port police and customs office in Psathi. Tel. 51332. Under construction opposite the jetty is a complex that will include a ticket office, café, and waiting room but until they complete it there is nowhere to shelter while waiting for the boat, as the café on the dock doesn't open for the convenience of passengers.

Road system

The few roads that exist here are of a better quality than you might expect and are being slowly extended in a project financed by a government grant. At the moment, the road from **Psathi** (the port) up to **Hora** (the village) is a cemented track in a reasonable state of repair.

From just above the port, and to the side of a house on the left that displays a rooms-to-let sign, a wide but rutted dirt road starts and continues to **Aliki**. This route is used by heavy lorries transporting minerals to the port.

From just below the village, to the left while looking down hill, is another dirt road that will eventually reach **Ta Prassa**. This track is narrow and in places covered by large loose stones which make even walking difficult on the slopes and it is necessary to walk sideways in some parts.

Buses There aren't any.

Taxis Four permits have been applied for but, as yet, not granted. In the meantime, two green three-wheelers serve as taxis and, as they meet all boats, if you place yourself in a strategic position on the road from Hora to Psathi they will take you and your luggage down. There is no vehicle rental.

Petrol There isn't any.

Maps There aren't any on sale in any of the shops unless someone has since taken up my suggestion but, judging by the reception this got, it seems unlikely. (Mr) Margaro Petraki has small photocopies of the large map kept in the president's office. He has a rooms-to-rent sign that displays his name outside his house at the top end of town. This map is splendidly out of date (1662, would you believe!) and is only inscribed in Greek, and of course it shows none of the roads. Because of this our own map doesn't show the exact routes as I am neither cartographer nor surveyor, but it should be accurate enough to give you the general idea.

Accommodation

At the time of writing, there are only four villagers with rooms to rent and between them there are sixty beds available.

Name	Tel. No.	Area
Margaro Petraki	51314	Hora
Nikolas Venturis	51329	Hora
Stephanos Melanitis	51220	15 metres up from the port
Georgis Pasamichalis	51340	Aliki

Camping
As the demand for beds in summer far outstrips the supply, camping is tolerated on the beaches.

Where to eat

There are five places to eat on the island, and you can also get a meal at the accommodation in **Aliki** where the owner cooks for his guests. **Psathi** has a taverna and a café. In **Hora,** two of the remaining establishments are roast-meat tavernas — one you may not normally pass in your wanderings is situated just downhill from the new school buildings. Standards are high and prices ridiculously cheap.

The café/taverna in the main street that has a multicoloured plastic fly dissuader in the doorway serves a continental breakfast.

Nightlife

Well, there is the "2002" pub in the village!

What to see and do

To pad out the possibilities, avoid reading the section on "Useful information" and make a list of the five tavernas, post office, telephone office, five shops, surgery, children's playground and police station, and then give yourself points when you find them!

Track down a donkey and guide to take you to **Palio Castro,** two hours from the village, and see the few large stones that are the surviving remains of the island's old capital.

Take a pleasant hike to **Aliki** and on to **Elliniko** if you have the stamina, where evidence exists that Kimolos and Milos were once joined. On the shoreline and below the sea lie the remains of a village with houses, tombs and sarcophagii in their watery graves.

The route to **Ta Prassa** passes a strange sight; there are the usual walled terraces everywhere but, in addition to these, are the same stones in huge heaps, and in places the very strata seem to be

(Opposite) *Amorgos. The Monastery of Khozoviotissa is a masterpiece of architecture and a tribute to the endurance of those who built it. (See page 68)*

composed completely of these rocks, giving the appearance that the hill side shattered into these smaller fragments. The water's edge is lined by very smooth rock that provides a comfortable surface for sunbathing.

There is a **museum** of sorts in one room of the old people's home and the key is held by Manolis Afendakis, whose daughter, Anna, is the matron there.

Useful information

Money matters The island has no banks and so there is only the post office to cash travellers' and Eurocheques. It's in the middle of the village and near the community office (sign reading "Kinotita"); be warned that this office may close early at 13.00 if the clerk is doing holiday relief and has to leave to catch the caique to Milos.

Police Just down from the larger red and silver domed church. Tel. 51205.

Telephone office Next to the Byzantine church in the middle of the village. Open from 07.45 to 14.15 Monday to Friday.

Health matters The doctor's surgery and pharmacy are at the lower end of town and on the only route up from the port. The building is identifiable by the small red cross on the sign. Tel. 51222.

Beaches

Kimolos has no shortage of beaches that are all of the sand and pebble variety. As previously mentioned, the road to **Ta Prassa** passes some very smooth rocks on the water's edge and two small tree-lined beaches. **Aliki** has long narrow beaches with low rocks behind them. There is a small pleasant sandy stretch in the **port** area.

(Opposite) *Vathi (Sifnos) is a beautiful bay where the sandy beaches are interrupted here and there by pretty houses and the quaint little church on the sea front.*

Kimolos. The main square at the highest end of the village.

Historical background

Kimolos has evidence of habitation dating back to the Mycaeanian period and excavations at **Elliniko** have unearthed artifacts from 2500BC when Kimolos, the islet of Aghia Andrea, and Milos were all one land mass.

The old capital was in the centre of the island and was seemingly far from well protected since not only did pirates visit the community, but they chose it as a home base from which to raid passing ships and set out to pillage other Cyclades islands.

Kimolos was once a major exporter of chalk but the supply of this mineral has long since been exhausted.

Polivos

Known by many names, including Poliavos and Polino, this island, although the home of shepherds a century ago, is now uninhabited. It was owned by Stavros Logothitis who bequeathed it to the church, a fact much lamented by the president of Kimolos.

On the fifteenth of August many people make the crossing from Kimolos to celebrate the festival of Panayiri at the only church there and every five years culling is necessary of the herds of wild goats that are found in abundance on its rocky landscape.

Many chartered yachts visit the sandy cove behind the tiny islet of Aghios Yiorgis but no caiques make the trip except at the time of the festival.

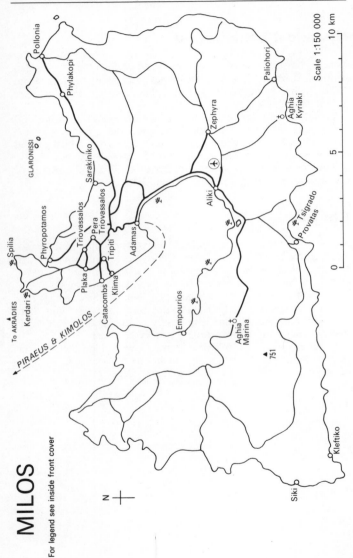

MILOS

For legend see inside front cover

Scale 1:150 000

0   5   10 km

FIFTEEN
Milos

Population: 4,500   Highest point: 883m
Area: 160 sq. km.   Hotel beds: 439

The largest of the south east Cyclades islands, Milos seems even larger than it actually is, as the approach from Sifnos by ferry views nearly half of the island's coast line. The harbour lies inside a long gulf which provides excellent shelter from both bad weather and detection by other shipping, and this has led to the port being used extensively throughout history. Another reason for shipping to visit Milos is to transport the rich mineral deposits of perlite, bentonite, kaolin, alanite, borite, silicates, manganese, lead, sulphur, obsidian and others that are widely exported. Evidence of their excavation dots the landscape and its white scars appear among the strangely coloured rocks yet undisturbed: the lunar-like projections at Sarakiniko, the almost blood red of the earth at the northern tip of the island, and the occasional pinky mauve rock that accentuates the blues and greens of the sea coves.

For such a large and fertile island, there are surprisingly few inhabitants and large areas have no villages at all. Another mystery is why Milos hasn't been more commercialised by the tourist industry, as it has everything that visitors could hope to find, including dozens of long sandy beaches, many of which have the unusual advantage of hot springs running through them to take the edge off early and late season chilly seas. Whatever the wind direction, there are always sheltered beaches, and entertainment facilities range from museums to discotheques providing something for most tastes.

Throughout the island, yellow signs by the road side forbid hunting (a very popular Greek Sunday pastime) and the airport displays posters advising arriving passengers that the island is the one remaining habitat of a rare species of snake and warning of the penalties for harming or exporting these creatures.

Arrival by sea

Milos is usually the last stop on the ferry route and the boats remain in port at **Adamas** overnight before retracing their course on the return to Piraeus. The number of islands visited en route makes the journey time ten hours or more. Routes are:

● Piraeus, Kythnos, Serifos, Sifnos, Milos.
● Milos, Folegandros, Santorini.
● Milos, Syros.

The first route also calls at Kimolos twice weekly and is a daily service. The last route only operates once a week. Tickets can be bought from travel offices in Adamas. The port police office is opposite the jetty and, as the island is one of the official entry ports to Greece, there is also a customs facility. Tel. 22100.

Caiques leave at 07.00 and 13.30 from the secondary port of **Pollonia** to make the thirty-minute crossing to Kimolos. Motor bikes are carried but no larger vehicles.

Arrival by air

The island's tiny airport is six kilometres from the main town of Plaka (also known as Hora), and the facilities include a snack bar and toilets. Olympic Airways flights from Athens are made by Dornier aircraft that seat nineteen passengers and the journey takes forty-five minutes. In season the usual morning and evening departures are boosted by an additional midday flight three times a week. Coaches transport passengers to and from the airport and leave from the Olympic Airways office, twenty metres from the square in Adamas on the road to Plaka (Hora). Fare 50 drachmas. Tel. 22380 and 22381 (airport).

Road system

The roads from the port **Adamas** (or Adamantas) to the upper villages and Pollonia are wide and well surfaced but unfortunately the quality is spoilt by a chronic lack of direction signs. For example there is no warning given at all of the turn-off to Pollonia and

Pahena, either to enable you to make up your mind which road you want to take or to warn you of traffic approaching from the right. Further along the Pollonia road is a fork to the right without a sign of any kind. If you take this fork you will come across another one fifteen metres later where, a little belatedly, an arrow labelled "Pollonia" directs you to complete the triangular detour and you finally learn that you were on the right road without turning off at all. During the day this solitary sign is visible but at night it can't be seen from any distance and so you may reach **Pollonia** seven kilometres away before you find out where the road leads.

Milos, Klima. This must be the most widely photographed area on the island and the variety of colour schemes of the paintwork is enchanting.

In addition to the routes to **Hora** and the eastern coastal edge, a road leads around the bay, passing endless beaches, until it reaches **Aghia Marina** where the asphalt ends and a wide dirt track continues to various isolated churches and beaches in the west. In places the gradient poses a problem for two-wheeled vehicles. Likewise the road from **Plaka** to **Phyropotamos** is horribly steep, although it has been well flattened by the lorries. To Plathiena, Kerdari, Skinopi and Kipos the journey must be completed on foot.

Town sign posts are in English as well as Greek but there aren't enough of them in the four villages (**Triovassalos, Pera Triovassalos, Plakes** and **Tripiti**) above Adamas to let you know when you leave one and enter another. Within these villages the placing of signs is such that they can only be viewed by traffic in one direction, hence the four settlements may be considered as one large village. There may however be occasions when you need to know more precisely where you are; for example it is easier to locate the road to the Catacombs from Tripiti than from Triovassalos. In this case I suggest that you stop a passerby and say the name of one of the villages and point to the ground, at which time they will hopefully agree or say the correct name of the area. If you get really lucky, you may be pointed in the direction you wish to go!

The last anomaly is **Zephyra** to which there are no sign posts whatever. Take the coast road from Adamas and when after five kilometres you pass the electricity generating station, you will be faced by two white arrows on blue backgrounds (looking remarkably like "one-way system" signs) and pointing in opposite directions. If you head left, the road leads to Zephyra. It isn't a one-way street, and neither is the road to the right. I can only assume that the two arrows have been placed there to discourage you from continuing in a straight line and therefore into the brick wall.

Buses There is a frequent service from **Adamas** to **Plaka** and at least three departures daily to and from **Pollonia**. There is a very infrequent service to **Aghia Marina**, enquire at the travel offices for current details.

The public buses are a light blue/green colour and not to be confused with the navy blue coaches that belong to the mineral ore extraction companies and which carry only company employees.

The little beach at Phyropotamos, Milos.

Taxis The island has eight taxis that meet both ferry and flight arrivals. The rank is in Adamas on the sea front, under the trees.
Petrol There are two petrol stations, the nearest to the port is 500 metres along the coast road and the other is found at the start of Triovassalos village. Both are well signposted.
Vehicle hire Cars and motorbikes can be hired in Adamas. Pollonia has a rent-a-bike business advertised at the bus stop.
Maps There are two maps and a guide book printed in English, French and German sold at the travel offices and many tourist shops. The two maps have a very similar cover but different colour shadings within the islands outline. The yellow one has more information on the front and is easier to read at a glance but the orange shaded map is more accurate and includes a guide to the ruins at Plaka. If you are colour blind, I suppose you will have to take pot luck!

The guide book is full of pretty colour photographs, church and archaeological site details and histories and makes a good souvenir at 600 drachmas a copy. The map it contains is in black and white and so placed that it is difficult to use without a bit of a fuss.

Accommodation

Hotels
Milos has a dozen hotels including one that describes itself as a "Holiday Village" and has a swimming pool, indoor and outdoor restaurants, bar and pool tables among its facilities. With the exception of the Panorama Hotel at Klima, all the hotels are in Adamas.

Hotel	Category	Tel. No.	Beds
Adamas	B	41844	22
Popi	B	21988	12
Venus Village	B	22020	173
Afrodite of Milos	C	22020	34
Chronis Bay	C	22226	32
Corali	C	22204	31
Meltemi	C	22284	24
Milos	C	22087	36
Delfini	D	22001	42
Georgantis	D	21955	19
Panorama (Klima)	D	21623	16
Semiramis	D	22118	29

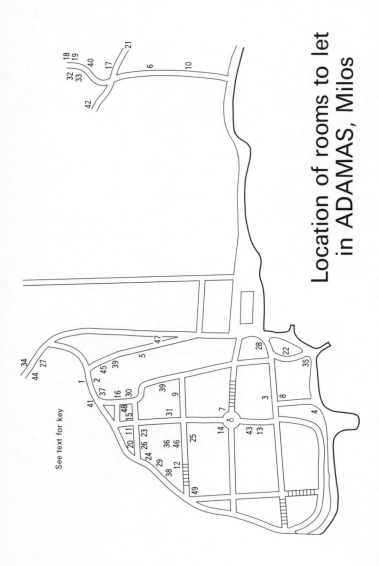

Location of rooms to let
in ADAMAS, Milos

See text for key

Rooms

Many of the houses in Adamas that have rooms to rent have no signs outside, so I have included a sketch map of their location.

Owner	Tel. No.	Map reference
Katina Afentaki	22119	1
Kostas Afentakis	22215	2
Maria Berdologou	22214	3
Eleni Braousogiani	22183	4
Manolis Braoudogianis	22183	5
Flora Drouga	22047	6
Anna Gozandinou	22364	7
Christina Xidou	-	8
Despina Xidou	-	9
Giorgos Xidous	22029	10
Ioulia Koureli	22184	11
Marigo Koureli	22227	12
Nontas Kourelis	22123	13
Katina Krisouli	-	14
Anna Kypreou	-	15
Eleni Lilli	22206	16
Christina Loukaki	22392	17
Yiannis Makrinos	22058	18
Anna Makrinou	22058	19
Marina Malli	22184	20
Antonia Marinitsi	22045	21
Katina Marotheodoraki	21970	22
Katina Marouditsi	-	23
Kaliopi Mathioudaki	22132	24
Yiannis Mathioudakis	22001	25
Stavros Mathioudakis	22132	26
Maria Mavroyianni	22151	27
Maria Mikeli	22167	28
Zafeiro Pastrikou	22239	29
Pavlos Pirounakis	22138	30
Thekla Pizu	22220	31
Fragoula Souli	22348	32
Sarantos Soulis	22031	33
Stella Sirmaleniou	22181	34
Antonio Themeli	22349	35
Anna Tseroni	22213	36
Antonis Tseronis	22002	37
Filipos Tseronis	22213	38

Owner	Tel. No.	Map reference
Stefanos Tseronis	21666	39
Evangelia Vamvarkari	-	40
Maria Vamvarkari	21765	41
Yiorgos Vamvarkaris	22123	42 & 43
Kostas Vamvounis	22150	44
Artemis Vichos	-	45
Dimitris Vichos	22185	46
Flora Vichou	-	47
Krissi Vichou	22211	48
Nikos Vikelis	21863	49

There are rooms available to rent in other areas, too. Names and telephone numbers are listed:

Pollonia

Maria Hatsigrigoriou	41396	Soultana Marinitsi	41346
Kostas Iliopoulos	41248	Yerasimos Marinitsis	41346
Androniki Kamakari	41226	Saron Mathioudaki	22127
Maria Kamakari	41317	Yiorgos Mavroyannis	41237
Nikoleta Kamakari	41276	Alexandros Petrakis	41222
Stella Katri	41242	Flora Tsamasfiri	41330
Manolis Katris	41259	Argyro Vamvouni	41249
Katina Kypreou	41256	Katina Vamvouni	41229
Maria Lilli	41208	**Hora**	
Tassos Lillis	41333	Yiannis Evripidis	21289
Antonia Malli	41245	Katina Katagouni	21401
Flora Malli	41210	Kostas Karagounis	21401
Dimitris Mallis	41380	Yiorgis Mallis	21528
Nikos Mallis	-	Petros Vikelis	21365
Stelios Mallis	-	**Emborio**	
Yiorgos Mallis	41209	Manolis Koliarakis	21389

Where to eat

The port has a variety of restaurants and one fast food establishment. In addition, there are two restaurants in Pollonia, a roast-meat taverna at Triovassalos, a restaurant at the hotel in Klima and a taverna in Zephyra. Recommended is the restaurant at the Hotel Milos in Adamas where the lack of atmosphere and decor are more than compensated for by the excellent food.

Nightlife

The island has two discotheques: the Venus is at the far end of the beach to the left of the jetty in Adamas (back to the sea); and the Apollonia is 100 metres before the fork in the road to Hora, where the road to Pollonia begins.

As well as a bar at the Hotel Venus, on the beach road and immediately behind the taxi rank is a café/bar where the many tables outside provide a pleasant setting for an after dinner tipple under the trees and within earshot of the waves.

What to see and do

Thermal baths

These natural saunas may help alleviate any cramped muscles gained from sleeping on the ferry or contoured mattresses! A visit to the **Provata** baths can be a good way to round off a day spent at the nearby beach. From the signpost at the fork where the track to the right leads to the beach, take the left hand path, which has been nicely flattened by the lorry whose driver lives next door to the baths, 200 metres from the fork. The road ends with a small hill on which a church has been converted for use as a house. Ten metres before the church and inside what looks remarkably like a half-built garage, are two rooms divided by a canvas curtain. The first is used as a changing room and the second houses the entrance to the short narrow tunnel that forms the baths. On days when the wind is from the south, the heat is dissipated and the effect is lost.

Other sites of thermal baths are found at **Aliki, Adamas, Skinopi** and **Paliohori**.

Museums

Milos has two museums both of which are in Plaka. The archaeological museum is a rather grand building and its entrance contains a reproduction of the Venus de Milo in pride of place. The exhibits are well labelled and attractively displayed. Admission is 300 drachmas (150 for students). Open from 08.15 to 13.30 Monday to Saturday and 09.30 to 12.30 on Sunday. The museum is located in the lower of the two squares in Plaka.

The folklore museum is signposted from both squares and is sited across a cobbled courtyard from the large church of Panayia Korfiatissa. It contains documents relating to the island's history and examples of local handicrafts which can be viewed between 10.00 and 12.00 on Wednesdays and Sundays in winter but during the same hours as the archaeological museum in season.

Boat trips

Milos Tours, in the port, offer two boat tours of the island. The longer trip calls at Kleftiko, Paliohori, Aghia Kyriaki (for lunch), Pollonia, Glaronissia, Plathiena and then back to Adamas. The cost is 1,500 drachmas exclusive of food, departure at 09.00 and return at 18.30.

A shorter trip lasting three hours and costing 1,000 drachmas visits Sikia and Kleftiko. The office can also advise you about caiques to Empourios (pronounced Ambourio) where there is a pleasant beach not accessible by road. A telephone at the taverna there can be used to summon a caique when you are ready to make the return trip.

Kleftiko

This area of coastline is riddled with caves and was the location of a pirate's lair.

Sikia

Here a large cave, accessible only by sea and large enough to enter by small boats, has a small sandy beach that gets light from where the roof has caved in.

Glaronissia

These small islets provide a popular roost for seagulls (from which they get their name) and are composed of rocks that resemble vertically packed stone crystals.

Ancient city

Just south of Tripiti the Dorians built a city between 1100 and 800 BC to replace the settlement at Phylakopi. The most notable feature of the excavations is the Roman amphitheatre, where seven rows of marble seating remain in good condition. The fields around the theatre are strewn with reddish brown stonework which, apart from a plaque marking the place where the Venus de Milo was found, are all that remains of the city.

Milos, Phyropotamos. The successor to the traditional Caique, but equally attractively painted, this speed-boat runs in a sheltered cove.

Catacombs

At the end of a wide, cemented road leading down from Tripiti and well signposted are the catacombs. From the parking area, progress is being made to complete a stepped and paved pathway in place of the difficult donkey track that leads to the entrance 300 metres further down the hill side. The catacombs have been attractively illuminated by many tiny mock oil lamps which helps preserve the atmosphere surrounding the 291 tombs. There is no admission fee and the door is open from 09.00 to 15.00 daily.

Phylakopi

Extensive excavations have been made of this, the first settlement on Milos, that was the location of three subsequent cities each built on the remains of the earlier city after it was destroyed by invaders. The construction covered a period of 1,500 to 2,000 years and the excavations have unearthed a Mycenaean temple and a multi-roomed palace as well as numerous artifacts. This area is well signposted, three kilometres from Pollonia on the road from Adamas.

Milos. The western tip of the island as seen from Plaka.

Useful information

Money matters Adamas has branches of the three largest **banks** along the waterfront road which is also the location of the **post office.** Normal bank opening hours may be extended in peak season for exchange transactions. Plaka also has a post office in the lower of its two squares.

Police The police station is in the higher of the two squares in Plaka. Tel. 21204.

Health matters The island is proud of its brand new **health centre** nearly opposite to the archaeological museum in the square in Plaka. Tel. 22100. There are at least three conspicuous **pharmacies** in Plaka and one in Adamas by the Olympic Airways office in the road to the upper villages.

Reading matter Books and magazines in English are sold at the shop opposite the kiosk on the sea front in Adamas.

Laundry There is a laundry/dry cleaners 500 metres from the jetty along the coast road towards Zephyra. In the high season they may be inundated with linen from the hotels so be sure to enquire how long the cleaning will take and then add on a few days to be on the safe side if you have a deadline to meet.

Telephone office The O.T.E. is on the sea front road in Adamas.

Centres of population

Adamas

Adamas (also known as Adamatas) is the largest of the island's two ports and is also the centre for tourism since all but one of the hotels are here, together with all the facilities a visitor could need. There are beaches within easy walking distance for those who don't wish to explore.

Looking inland as the ferry nears the port, to the left is a sandy tree-lined beach whose most noticeable feature is a large boat that has been dry docked there. The beach is backed by many hotels that line the route uphill to the main village. At the base of the residential area, the sea front road houses shops, ticket offices, restaurants and the banks. After forking by the side of two more hotels where the road to Plaka begins, the road continues along the edge of the bay and passes many sandy beaches before reaching a junction where a road to the left curves up to join the route to Plaka. As well as the attractrive beaches on one side, the road has many warehouses and processing plants that play a part in the export of minerals, and the many jetties that intersperse the sandy stretches are for loading the ore-carrying vessels.

One of the most pleasant areas of the village is the small square where buses and taxis wait under the trees. A large café on the waterfront is a popular place for a cool drink at all times of day.

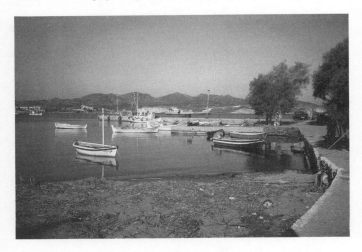

Milos Pollonia. The island's second port whence the journey may be made to neighbouring Kimolos (just visible in the background of the photograph).

Plaka

Plaka, also known as Hora, is the island's capital, five kilometres from Adamas. It is the most traditional of the settlements and has some attractive houses in the side streets, built in the typical Cycladic style of architecture. Two squares are the most useful points for orientation. The first is reached at the end of the road up from Tripiti and after passing the museum and health centre the road ascends further and curves to the left to enter the second square.

Triovassalos, Pera Triovassalos, Plakes

These villages form a large residential and commercial centre. As mentioned in the "Road system" section, the villages are poorly signposted and the boundaries are indistinguishable, which means that the area might be better considered as one small town rather than as separate communities. Little of appeal is found here unless you wish to see a football match at the large stadium.

Pollonia

While quite ugly on its outskirts, this village becomes very picturesque at its coastal edge, where brightly painted caiques moored in the shallows by a sandy beach provide an attractive view that can be appreciated while taking a meal at one of the tavernas on the quayside.

Two tavernas, a bar, a shop and a few rooms to rent comprise the facilities. From here caiques leave twice daily to make the short crossing to Kimolos, visible across the bay.

Klima

A few houses and one hotel are all that mark this tiny hamlet but the area is much visited because of its boatsheds! Not as extraordinary as it may sound, as the boatsheds are incorporated as the lower storey of houses, and each has been painted a different colour. This, together with the nets draped over balcony railings, makes for one of the most attractive sights in Greece and visitors to the island are sure to see at least one poster of Klima during their stay, if not the real thing.

Zephyra

Though hard to believe, this was once the island's capital until plagues and earthquakes forced its residents to leave. One large church and a café/taverna are the only buildings of note and it has no charm whatsoever.

Beaches

Where shall I start! The island is packed with beaches to appeal to all tastes: the sandy-edged millpond type, the breaker type, and the snorklers' and divers' dream variety are all found in abundance. If the wind is from the north, the southern coast line will be sheltered and vice versa.

I will list only the most notable and those with facilities or unusual features. From Adamas, clockwise, you have: **Plathenia,** sandy; **Spilia,** sandy beaches and many caves with strangely coloured cliff edges; **Sarakiniko,** little sandy beaches tucked amongst peculiar white rocks looking like something from another world; **Phyropotamos,** a very pretty deep cove where the greens and blues of the sea are edged by pinky mauve rocks and a sandy beach; **Paliohori** and **Aghia Kyriaki** perhaps the best beaches — the east beach at Paliohori has reddish sand and a taverna; **Tsigrados,** white sand and crystal clear sea; **Empourios** reached by caique from Adamas, with a taverna; **Mavra Gremna** and **Aliki,** with warmer than usual seas due to the hot springs that surface there.

Historical background

The origin of the island's name is not certain but has been attributed to an early settler, Milo, who was a descendent of the King of Cyprus.

Milos was colonised by the Minoans, Mycenaeans and possibly the Phoenicians, who found a wealth of obsidian, a black mineral that could be honed or chipped to give a good cutting edge and so was invaluable for tool making. These implements have been found throughout the Mediterranean which shows that the island traded extensively as far back as 5000BC.

At Phylakopi, excavations have unearthed the oldest neolithic settlement in the Cyclades. The majority of later (1100 BC) colonists were Dorians who enraged the Athenians by siding with the Spartans in the Peloponnesian War and consequently, after a third attempt at invasion of Milos, the Athenians were successful and killed all the male inhabitants and sold the women and children into slavery. Five hundred mainlanders remained to form a colony. With the help of the Spartans, the surviving islanders took advantage of the fall of Athens and resettled and prospered until attacks by pirates caused them to seek protection from the Romans who, in response, founded a city at Klima, where their amphi-theatre can be seen today.

The Venetians ruled the island from 1207 to 1566 and suppressed several attempts at insurrection. Their rule ended when the Turks conquered the Cyclades; but Milos was not occupied by the victors who instead collected taxes by means of "Commissioners", elected from the local noblemen, who also presided over minor judicial matters. More serious cases were decided by the Sultan's Kapudan Pasha. During this time, the island was continually attacked by pirates and one, Ioannis Kapsis, had himself crowned King of Milos and ruled for three years until he was executed in Constantinople in 1680. Some islanders emigrated to England and were welcomed by the Duke of York. The houses they were given formed what is still called "Greek Street" in London's Soho district.

Milos was among the first of the islands to participate in the 1821 revolution and it was within its harbour that ships from Spetses destroyed the Turkish fleet.

Although many finds from Milos can be seen in museums both in Athens and abroad, the most famous artifact is the Venus de Milo which was discovered on 8 April 1820 by George Betonis, a farmer, who had spotted a hollow area under some stones while planting corn. The statue (in two pieces) was revealed and a French cadet, who is said to have been passing by at the time the find was made, guessed the value of the discovery; word eventually reached Marcello, an embassy secretary, who immediately set sail for Milos to purchase the statue. By the time he arrived, the Venus was already sold and being loaded into a caique and it took a lot of hard bargaining before the statue was finally bought for the French ambassador to Constantinople. He presented it to Louis XVIII who in turn presented it to the Louvre Museum where is can be seen today, minus the arms which were lost somewhere along the line.

Antimilos

Antimilos (or Erimomilos) is an uninhabited island to the north-east of Milos. It is preserved as a National Game Reserve, and known for a species of wild Chamois not found anywhere else in the world, which lives there undisturbed. Rainwater collects in special storage tanks for the animals and at times of food shortage drops are made by aircraft.

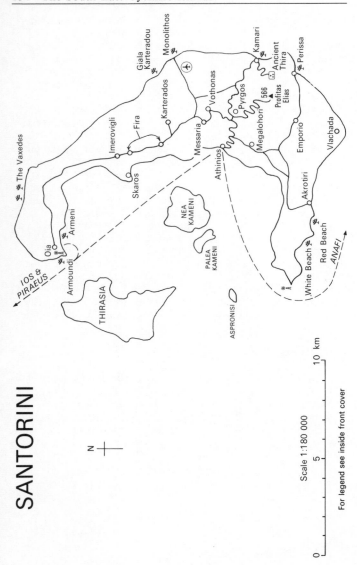

SANTORINI

N

Scale 1:180 000

For legend see inside front cover

0   5   10 km

SIXTEEN

Santorini (Thira)

Population: 7,500   *Highest point: 567m*
Area: 75 sq. km.   *Hotel beds: 1,000 +*

As long as the ferry arrives in daylight, there is no possibility of mistaking Santorini for any other island, nor, arguably, anywhere else on earth. With its precipitous rocky cliffs rising sheer from the waves in multilayers of browns, reds, black, beige and white, with the odd green tinge from sparse plant life precariously surviving in this cruel environment, it resembles what it is: a scarred wound of one of nature's most dramatic disruptions.

The intense blue of the sea is a clue to its incredible depth that once caused it to be charted as "bottomless" and makes it impossible for ships to anchor off a large proportion of its coastline. The three settlements of **Oia, Fira** and **Pyrgos** together with the more remote villages in all their dazzling whiteness are in stark contrast to the astonishingly dark landscape they perch on.

The nearest islet of Nea Kameni is edged with demonically black boulders, seemingly lubricated where the white foam breaks on them. As you near the little port of **Athinios,** it becomes ever more obvious that to ascend the cliff face is going to take quite some doing and there will probably be a few vehicles making the last minute descent and whose progress you can watch as they tackle the steep zig-zagging road.

There can be very few people who haven't already seen a view of the sun setting behind the volcano, albeit unwittingly, as it must be one of the most photographed displays in the world. Similarly, the island's black sand beaches show off to great effect the multi-coloured bikinis of bathers and the garishly painted pedaloes, to make a far more photogenic scene than on shores with sand of the conventional hue.

Santorini is not new to tourism and while Fira and at least two other resorts have done everything possible to provide all facilities for visitors, the National Tourist Organisation of Greece has imposed strict regulations concerning conservation and development, in order to maintain Oia as a traditional Greek village. The islanders accept and enjoy tourism, and an airport large enough to receive international flights was completed several years ago, enabling charter flights to bring in "package" holidaymakers who have chosen to spend all or half of their vacation here as part of a two-centre holiday.

Also covered in this chapter is the tiny island of Thirasia, usually visited as part of a day-trip to the volcanic islands. Thirasia and Santorini are exact opposites and the opportunity exists to visit a totally uncommercialised and incredibly pretty Greek village above the port, perhaps to speculate on how the larger island of Santorini once was.

Santorini is much described as having many ruins still remaining from the last serious disaster, the earthquake of 1956; but apart from incomplete buildings of yellowing cement embedded with small stones — which contrast unfavourably with the inhabited dwellings, carefully maintained in brilliant white or attractive pastel combinations — nowhere on the island, to my mind, still bears any obvious signs of the devastation that occurred.

Arrival by sea

Santorini is a popular destination with the shipping lines, despite the smallness of its port, **Athinios.** Only two ferries can dock at any one time and this sometimes means that a third ferry has to wait a short while for a berth. Routes from Santorini are:

● Piraeus, Syros, Paros, Naxos, Ios, Santorini.
● Piraeus, Folegandros, Santorini.
● Santorini, Anafi, Crete, Kassos, Karpathos, Rhodes.

There are at least three daily departures for Piraeus in summer, dwindling to just one in the off season. The journey time direct is ten hours and all departures are from the port of Athinios (the stress is on the "o"). It should be noted that the port is ten kilometres from Fira and you should allow sufficient time before the boat departure to get you there. For every departure and arrival, at least one local bus leaves from the main square in Fira two hours before the advertised ship arrival time. If you intend to use this bus to get to the port, it is best to err on the side of caution and set out even earlier, as the buses regularly leave before the scheduled time and "sardines in a tin" is an inadequate cliché to describe the way they pack in all-comers, throwing the luggage on top. If you find you have missed the bus for an early morning boat, there may be no taxis around to help you make last minute dash.

High speed catamarans usually depart from Athinios but also use on occasions the small port below Fira, so be sure to ask about the departure port when buying the ticket. Catamaran routes are:

● Santorini, Crete.
● Santorini, Naxos, Ios, Paros, Mykonos.

These vessels don't run in bad weather and tickets are roughly double the price of those for ferries, but the journey time is more than halved.

All vehicles must have a ticket before embarkation is allowed; there is one travel office in the port and an agent who is always there outside of normal shop hours. It isn't advisable to depend on this type of last minute ticket purchase in season, however, as boats do become fully booked especially around public holidays.

Once a week there is a mail boat to Anafi that carries passengers, but it is very difficult to get any information on this vessel. Try the port police: Tel. 22239, or call at their office on the left as the main road leaves Fira for Oia.

Arrival by air

Santorini has an airport that can take the larger aircraft used by charter flight companies. International arrivals come from: Gatwick, Manchester, Paris, Dusseldorf, Stockholm, Monaco, Brussels, Milan, Vienna and Satlzburg. For those wishing to fly direct to Santorini, the arrangements are the same as those for charter flights to Athens (see page 21).

Domestic flights in summer arrive from: Athens (3 a day), Crete (3 a week), Rhodes (4 a week) and Mykonos (daily). The offpeak season timetable is changed monthly.

The Olympic airways office is at the bottom of the main vertical road in Fira, ten metres to the right. Office hours are from 08.00 to 14.30 daily. Tel. 22493 and 22793, airport 22218. This is also where the Olympic Airways buses leave from, to meet each flight and take passengers for departures. The fare is 70 drachmas for the seven-kilometre journey to Monolithos, where the airport consists of a small waiting lounge that they don't bother to open in good weather. There is a post box for last minute postcards and very little else besides the military base. (See Monolithos page 150 for accommodation details.)

Road system

First impressions of road standards depend on whether you arrive by sea or air. From the port of **Athinios** the road that ascends to join the main road is of concrete, and at its tight corners the surface has deteriorated to leave some quite deep pot-holes. If you are in the bus you will probably be too busy speculating on whether the bus can negotiate the turns to concern yourself about the odd pot-hole! If, however, like me, you arrive with trusty moped, you will be consumed by thoughts of just how recently you had the brakes checked, and fretting over how the engine is labouring on the climb even in first gear, and how on earth that truck is going to pass you without forcing you over the side! Get the picture? This delightful track joins the main road at a T-junction and from there the road is asphalted as far as **Fira.**

Finding Fira ia another matter as it isn't signposted until you reach it. At the top of the road from the port, follow the road to the left that bears a sign "Camping". To the right are **Megalohori, Emborio, Perissa** and **Akrotiri.** The next confusion is at another junction of three roads, where a sophisticated looking sign has arrows in directions that bear no relation at all to what you see around you. Coming from Athinios the sudden right ascends to **Pyrgos** and the left hand road continues on to **Fira.** Some warning of this junction is given only by "EKO" petrol station signs, otherwise you find yourself having passed it and then trying to find somewhere to stop and work out if you went the right way.

At **Messaria**, by way of a change, there are three roads to choose from and everything except Fira is signposted. Continue straight and then bear slightly to the right but watch out because there is another major road joining from the right and no warning signs.

I asked directions in the port and was told just to follow the asphalted road. This was extremely unhelpful as at each intersection, all branches were of the same surface. The next time I asked the direction to Fira, I was told it was "behind the moon".

I thought he was being facetious and replied that I hadn't got wings until I noticed that he was right, a full moon was right over one of the distant clusters of lights. The only potential problem, having eventually reached Fira, is that twenty metres after the first travel office "Maria Tours", where the road has a turn-off downhill to the right, you enter a one-way system and to get back to this area you have to drive full circle, turning just after the new hospital building and again in front of the new museum building.

The road from Fira or **Oia** gets off to a promising start but then narrows and the surface has crumbled in places. With the inevitable sheer drop down one side, it gets a bit hairy when a car needs to pass a bike, and must require considerable care when two larger vehicles meet.

There is an alternative route from Fira to Oia but except for the first kilometre out of Oia, where a new-looking concrete road leaves the town from the bus station fork, it is a dirt road and in places the accumulated sand makes road holding very bad. It also has some steep ascents before it reaches Fira and emerges at the turning marked "Oikismos and Exo Katikia".

The many tracks between **Vlachada, Perissa** and **Kamari** are a similar challenge and motor bikes other than the Enduro type find themselves going every which way but forward in the patches of deep sand.

Roads in all the villages and towns are concreted but it is possible to find yourself in the middle of a group of tiny houses where the road gets narrower and narrower until it suddenly becomes stepped, without your ever having passed a no-entry sign.

Buses

Buses leave from the square in **Fira** and timetables are posted on the left-hand side facing downhill and in most of the travel offices. In **Oia** buses leave from the parking area at the end of the right-hand fork of the main road leading into the town. Throughout the island, stops are clearly marked with the usual "Stassis" sign.
The routes are:

- Fira, Imerovigli, Oia. 08.30 to 22.30 hourly.
- Fira, Karterados, Messaria, Vothonas, Pyrgos, Megalohori, Emborio, Perissa. 07.30 to 22.30 hourly.
- Fira, Karterados, Messaria, Kamari. 07.30 to 21.00 half hourly.
- Fira, Karterados, Messaria, Vothonas, Pyrgos, Megalohori, Akrotiri. Mornings only.
- Fira, Karterados, Messaria, Vothonas, Pyrgos, Athinios.

The last route has departures two hours before each ferry arrival and occasionally even earlier. A seemingly impossible number of people are crammed into each vehicle on this route and luggage is thrown onto the shallow rack on the roof. It is wise to make sure all cases and back packs are securely closed and any attachments well attached. Anything fragile might be better taken into the bus with you.

Taxis
Taxis wait in the square in Fira, the port of Athinios, and at the airport. Reservations Tel. 22492 or from travel offices (who of course take a commission).

Petrol
There are three petrol stations on Santorini, at Fira, at Pyrgos, and just outside Kamari. All are well signposted. They open from 08.30 to 19.00 hours and operate a rota system to ensure that one is open until midnight.

Vehicle rental
The centre of Fira has numerous signs advertising car and bike rental agencies. Cars can also be found at Kamari and Oia but elsewhere only mopeds. Be absolutely sure the brakes work before you accept the vehicle, as you will certainly need them.

Useful information

Police The police station is along the main road in the Oia direction and a small signpost seems to point you further that way, but you are meant to descend the small alley that starts at the base of the sign. The offices are contained in one of the houses at the bottom and are identifiable only by the flag pole outside. Tel. 22649.

Port police Just opposite the covered market stall and five metres from the police sign is the port police office. Tel. 22239.

Telephone office This is at the top of the main pedestrian-only street in Fira and twenty metres to the left. While the long opening hours (07.45 to 21.45 Monday to Saturday) are realistic, there are only five booths, while collect and credit card calls must be made before 14.00 which may not be convenient when considering international time zones.

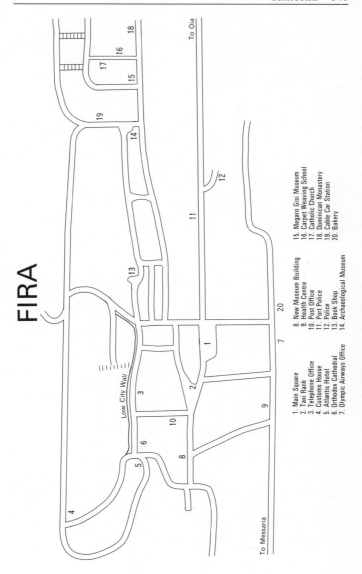

FIRA

To Oia

To Messaria

Low City Wall

1. Main Square
2. Taxi Rank
3. Telephone Office
4. Customs House
5. Atlantis Hotel
6. Orthodox Cathedral
7. Olympic Airways Office

8. New Museum Building
9. Health Centre
10. Post Office
11. Port Police
12. Police
13. Book Shop
14. Archaeological Museum

15. Megaro Gisi Museum
16. Carpet Weaving School
17. Catholic Church
18. Dominican Monastery
19. Cable Car Station
20. Bakery

Money matters The three main banks all have branches in or around Fira's main square and are well signposted. The post office is not so visible as it displays little of the characteristic yellow paintwork but it is situated behind "Maria Tours", on the far corner of the main square (looking away from Oia) and next door to the National Bank. Open from 07.45 to 14.15 Monday to Friday.

Laundry Although there are signs in English at Messaria advertising laundry facilities, they only take in linen from the hotels. When I called to ask the opening hours of the laundry in Fira ten metres down on the right hand side of the one-way street, the owner told me that he was selling up and moving to the mainland; but I include it here in case the next owner decides to continue in the same line of work, for there is a definite demand.

Reading matter At the top of the main pedestrian-only street in Fira, turn right and continue until faced by a raised marble verandah as the pavement turns to the right. Here there is a small book shop selling books and newspapers in English, German and French.

Fira

Sometimes written as "Thira", this town is the island's capital and is full of amenities for visitors. The small square is speckled with signs for "Fast food", travel offices and the bright colours of souvenir shops. Three small pedestrian-only cobbled streets ascend from the square to the city wall at the top where a long path leads up to the cable car station on the right and down to the Orthodox Cathedral on the left. Looking down from this path is the breathtaking view of the volcano caldera. Benches have been strategically placed and the wall kept low so that it's the ideal spot to view the sunset behind this spectacular setting. Below the wall, closely packed traditional houses hug the cliff face and their dazzling white is attractively interspersed with gentle pastels. The most common use of the buildings on the town side of the wall, however, seems to be for the high class jewellery shops that outnumber tavernas and souvenir shops two to one! Surprisingly there aren't a similar number of heel repair shops, for the glossy stones that make up the surface of the small streets aren't very even; only the most sensible shoes are practical. Whether or not they wear walking boots, Fira receives an "up-market" class of tourist in greater proportion to the back packers who perhaps head for the less expensive islands, and the bars and restaurants reflect this in their sophistication.

Accommodation in Fira

Beds on Santorini are very expensive compared to smaller islands. While there is a large selection of all types of accommodation in Fira, it isn't often situated in the centre of town, which makes it difficult to track down a room without instructions. Because of this, I recommend haggling with the hotel and pension owners at the port, and if your selection is one that has its own mini bus you will also save yourself the bus or taxi fare from the port. If you arrive in Fira without having secured a room, the many travel offices will try to find a vacancy, in return for commission, of course.

Hotels	Category	Telephone	Beds
Atlantis	A	22230	46
Villa Renos	B	22369	13
Antonia	C	22879	20
Kalisti Thira	C	22317	64
Kavalari	C	22455	39
Panorama	C	22481	34
Pelican	C	23113	34
Theoxenia	C	22740	20
Leta	D	22540	22
Lucas	D	22480	35
Santorini	D	22593	46
Tataki	D	22389	18
Assimina	E	22034	26
Katris	E	22842	15
Lignos	E	23101	15
Thirasia	E	22546	33

Rooms Usually referred to as "pansions", rooms in these family owned houses offer a generally cheaper alternative to the hotels, but private bathrooms are more rarely found in this category. Many such establishments are congregated on the road that passes the Olympic Airways office and on towards Oia. The Dominican convent has eleven rooms for visitors, who have the use of kitchen facilities and who should bear in mind that the front door is locked at 23.00 hours.

Youth hostels There are two youth hostels in Fira almost opposite each other and well signposted just past the convent. Both have facilities for eating breakfast and snacks on the premises.

Camping There are no campsites either official or otherwise in Fira. See Kamari and Perissa.

Where to eat
The eating places in Fira range from fast food take-aways to a fairly famous international restaurant. Unfortunately, in my opinion, there isn't much in between the two extremes. There are a few restaurants along the route to the cable car station that display some Greek dishes in illuminated glass cases to tempt your fancy if you are not attracted by any of the meats and sea food that are used to make up various types of *souvlaki*. Apart from these, there is only one traditional Greek taverna in the town.

In the side street opposite the entrance to "Mikes Pub", Nicholas has his moderately sized, drably decorated establishment. He opens the door at 19.30 or whenever he feels like it and the queue starts to form around 19.15 even in the quieter months.

By 19.40 he is already extremely crotchety and perspiring profusely, all the tables will be occupied, and when would-be diners stop him and announce that they seek a table for two, he will look at them in complete exasperation and ask if they can't see that the restaurant is full. Rather than wait, they then usually ask other diners if they might use unoccupied seats which causes further complaints when he has to make out two separate bills for one table.

The menu is chalked on a blackboard in Greek only and it's indecipherable even if you can read that language quite well, which gives him an opportunity to rattle off the six dishes on offer at an alarming speed and then fix you with a look that dares you to ask him to repeat it! I can vouch that this behaviour has nothing to do with the amount of work he has to do, as I had occasion to visit Santorini four years ago in February when I and the only other seven foreigners on the island would congregate in this taverna in the evenings to discuss our respective excursions. Each time another couple came into the restaurant, he would look towards heaven and "tut" loudly before going back into the kitchen for his note pad. I must add that we had given him no cause to resent our custom, having eaten, behaved and paid well on all our visits. As far as I am concerned, this all adds to the charm of the place and the food is really excellent. This time I was delighted to find a delicious dish, made with capers, that I had never heard of before, despite many years of residence in Greece.

One of the *souvlaki* restaurants has obviously gone to great lengths to provide entertainment for its customers and can subsequently guarantee "Nightly Sunsets" as displayed on their advertisement!

Night life
There are three discotheques in Fira: Enigma, Casablanca and the Town Club, plus numerous bars with various gimmicks including two music video bars.

Other centres of population

Oia
No stay on Santorini would be complete without at least a visit to Oia. This village at the far north of the island is the subject of strict laws imposed by the National Tourist Organisation of Greece to ensure that it remains unchanged by commercialisation and loses none of its traditional charm.

From the two-storey mansion houses built by wealthy seafarers to the *skafta* (houses which incorporate the mountain side into their structure) the buildings are incredibly picturesque both from the point of view of colour scheme and architectural design.

One main road leads to Oia and then, on the edge of the settlement, it divides and vehicles must follow the route to the right which leads to a large car park where the buses wait. Branching from this road is a wider concreted road that follows the coast line past many tiny and isolated beaches until it re-emerges in Fira. The left fork is for pedestrians and tricycles only and forms the main street of the village, passing hotels, the post office, museum, banks, shops and cafés.

The absence of large signs advertising various businesses is refreshing, as is the whole atmosphere of Oia, which is described in one guide book as "making you sensitive to poetry". The paths to the two main beaches in the area are signposted as they branch off from the main street, and the routes are stepped; so too is the path to the little port at Oia, another very attractive sight especially when viewed from a little way out to sea.

Many visitors to Santorini prefer this part of the island, which seems to offer a much more relaxing environment than they can find in Fira, although the amenities are still here for those that want them. The village even has two discotheques but they have been sited very discreetly.

Visitors have the opportunity to stay in one of the refurbished *skafta,* as E.O.T. and some private companies have houses for rent, both for long and short periods, and with varying numbers of bedrooms to suit couples, families and large groups. Places to stay are:

Hotels	Category	Tel. No.	Beds
Perivolas	A	71308	14
Laouda	B	71204	20
Fregata	D	71221	40
Anemones	E	71220	19
Atlantis Villas	B	71214	
E.O.T.	B	71234	
Perivolas	B	71308	

All of the boat trips to the volcano stop at Oia for at least two minutes before returning to Fira, so you have the option of disembarking here. This allows you enough time to wander around the little streets, visit the art gallery, see the museum exhibits (if you hurry), do some shopping, and still have time to enjoy a cocktail while watching the sunset from this romantic setting, before catching the bus back to Fira.

Kamari

Developed after the earthquake in 1956, Kamari is a modern resort centred on the famous black beach where the peculiar hue of the sand is highlighted even more by the incredible azure of the sea. Restaurants, bars, discos and shops line the road that verges the beach, and everything is on hand to cater for the many visitors who flock here each year. There is plenty of accommodation in Kamari:

Hotels	Category	Tel. No.	Beds
Sunshine	B	31394	68
Akis	C	31154	27
Artemis Beach	C	31198	54
Kamari	C	31243	104
Orion	C	31182	40
Poseidon	C	31387	60
Zephyros	C	31309	44
Akropoli	D	31012	30
Aspro Spiti	D	31441	29
Blue Sea	D	31481	49
Golden Sun	D	31301	30
Nikolina I	D	31253	64
Sigalas	D	31260	23

Ta Kymata	D	-	42
Dyonyssios	E	31310	16
O Ghiannis	E	31166	16
Kuramlengos	E	-	30
Nikolina II	E	31253	17
Nina	E	-	24
Prekamaria	E	31266	20
Villa Elli	E	31266	

Pensions and furnished apartments

Belonia Villas	A	31138
Anapliotis Elias		31256
Andrea		31314
Antonis		31385
Argo		31412
Asteria		31002
Christofora		31485
Kafouros		31493
Kapetan Ghiannis		31154
Katrakis		31313
Loizos		31307
Margarita		31437
Markakis		31468
Mendrinos		31258
Sirigos		31004
Sophia Janne		31005
Tragarakis		31487
Vailas		31482
Villa Astro		31366
Villa Irene		31145
Zaharakis		31252

Camping There is a campground on the left of the main road as it enters Kamari from Exo Gonia and fifteen minutes walk from the beach.

Perissa

This is a smaller resort than Kamari but with a longer beach (8kms!), again composed of black sand. The area is developing and a youth hostel, hotels and pensions have been built along the road side until, on reaching the edge of the beach at right angles, the road turns left and restaurants and tavernas pack the route and offer a pleasant setting in which to enjoy a meal. Somewhat ahead of their time perhaps are the roller skating rink and mini-golf that provide an outlet for any energy you may have left after a day on the beach.

The most conspicuous building by far is the church of Timios Stavros (Holy Cross), the largest church on the island, with its five aquamarine domes giving the sea considerable competition for the most intense colour.

The village sits at the base of Mesa Vouno (Inner Mountain), an enormous and atypical rock mass — it was in situ before the great eruptions and is not of volcanic composition. Where the beige rock and the black sand meet, a sharp contrast is formed by both extremes of geological colour scheme.

There are seven hotels in Perissa:

Hotels	Category	Tel. No.	Beds
Santa Irini	C	81301	23
Christine	D	81362	16
Zorzis	D	81244	19
Boubis	E	81203	29
Maroussina	E	-	12
Nota	E	81209	12
Perissa	E	-	32

The black sands of Perissa beach seen from the archaeological site of Ancient Thira. (Photo R. J. Thomas)

Youth hostel The Perissa Youth Hostel is on the left hand side of the main road into the village, about 700m from the beach.

Camping The camp site in Perissa boasts many facilities for the use of its guests, including restaurant, bar, tent hire and the usual amenities. As the main road reaches the beach and veers left, the camping ground is on the right hand corner.

Useful addresses The post office and telephone office are both located within a small grocer's shop on the square behind the large church. Another metered phone is available at the Retsina Taverna.

Messaria

Messaria is an inland village and perhaps an unlikely place for any commercialisation except that it straddles the crossroads of all the island's main routes. As well as new hotels, restaurants and tavernas, the area has many vineyards and two wine cellars where the produce can be tasted.

There are several hotels in Messaria:

Hotels	Category	Tel. No.	Beds
Anny	C	23102	48
Artemidoras	C	22502	30
Loizos	C	22359	23
Apollon	D	22906	24
Andreas	E	23154	28
Messaria	E	22594	13

Pyrgos

The word "Pyrgos" usually refers to a tower or castle but today there is very little remaining of the old castle walls above the village. The locals here proclaim that when all the rest of the island sinks in another eruption of the volcano, only Pyrgos will remain above sea level. Indeed it would have to be an almighty upheaval to submerge the summit of Profitas Elias, the mountain that overlooks the village. The streets within this village deserve inspection, and so too, I am told, do the interiors of the many churches but, alas, in the past, light-fingered visitors have made off with the icons, and now all doors are kept securely locked.

Emporio

Emporio at first sight has little to distinguish it from many other of the island's villages. However, if you wander in an up-hill direction through the maze of little streets, you reach an area of very traditional houses and may be lucky enough to get a glimpse of one of the usually unseen aspects of Greek life: black-clad old ladies, with scarves covering the lower part of their faces, sit in the doorways of their tiny homes and work at their lacemaking while talking energetically to all the neighbours who may be similarly occupied.

The name of the village implies a commercial centre, which it once was, both in milling corn and as a residential base for fishermen who set out from Perissa.

Karterados

This village is sited in a valley below the level of the main Fira to Messaria road, and thus is an exception to the general rule in Santorini which locates settlements high on top of a hill. As if to make a habit of unconventionality, the dome of the Church of the Ascension is painted jade green, completely out of step with all the others and their sky blue roofs. Accommodation in Karterados is provided by several hotels:

Hotels	Category	Tel. No.	Beds
Santorini Tennis Club	B	22122	22
Babis	D	22314	43
Cyclades	D	22948	32
Olympia	D	22213	56
Palladion	D	22583	22
Gina	E	22834	20
O Chiannis	E	22552	12

Monolithos

Monolithos is the closest village to the airport where the perimeter encloses a few reception buildings and an army base. The most noticeable feature is the lump of rock on the east side of the runway, on which sits the inevitable tiny church, and together they look very out of place beside the usually bustling airport.

This area contains the nearest beaches to Fira. Rooms are available at Kostas Bungalows, Tel. 22211, where there are 32 beds.

Akrotiri

Much visited because of its beaches and the excavations, the village has two restaurants and a wine-tasting cellar (see Things to see and do, page 152). Hotel Akrotiri, Tel. 31295, has 30 beds.

What to see and do

Archaeological Museum, Fira

This modern building has an attractive courtyard where the overhead security grid has had to be tailored to permit a palm tree to continue its growth. Inside are the usual assortment of pots and vases that look almost as good as the reproductions on sale in the souvenir shops. It opens 08.45 to 15.00 Monday to Saturday (closed Thursdays), Sunday 09.30 to 13.30. Tickets 200drs (100 for students). No photographs allowed. Situated next to the cable car entrance and well signposted.

Megaron Gyzi Museum, Fira

This charmingly converted mansion and its courtyard display exhibits that include many old photographs, documents, maps and newspaper clippings depicting the history of Santorini through its various volcanic eruptions and earthquakes. In a neighbouring and less modernised meeting hall where talks, plays and concerts are held, there is a permanent display of oil paintings in a very atmospheric setting. It is open 10.30 to 14.30 and 17.00 to 19.00 daily. Admission 150drs (100 for students). You will find it 10 metres further uphill than the carpet weaving school and the youth hostels.

Maritime Museum, Oia

This small building houses among other things, some remarkably well preserved figureheads from the old sailing ships. It is open from 1.00 to 11.30 and 16.00 to 17.00 hours.

Dominican Convent to The Sisters of Mercy, Fira

On the door of both the grounds of the nunnery and the church is a sign in English inviting those who wish to confess to a priest to ring the door bell. I was rather hesitant as this gave me no idea as to whether the area was open to the public, apart from to those with a troubled conscience. Gathering my courage, I rang and was admitted by Sister Hope who, of the ten resident nuns, is the only one with permission to have any contact with the outside world, since the order is a closed, though not silent, one.

This remarkable lady had spent forty years in the convent and talked to me about the changes that the years had brought to

Santorini. She showed me the icon of St. John the Baptist and some modern icons made within the nunnery. When we came to the room used by the nuns for meetings with family or those seeking guidance, I was moved. A barred screen separates the two halves of the room and in a corner is a turntable where objects may be placed for transfer to the other section. It was so prison-like and my sadness must have shown because Sister Hope went on to explain that the life wasn't one of misery or loneliness but of great joy filled with love for God. She was so sincere and radiated so much enthusiasm for what she was saying, that once again I was moved close to tears, and left there feeling much the richer for my visit.

The resident priest is Spanish and in fact Sister Hope and he are the only Greek-speaking people on the premises, as the other sisters are from El Salvador and Brazil so Spanish is the language used within the grounds.

The nunnery has eleven rooms for visitors who pay a charge of 600drs a night. An English woman who stayed there described being awoken every morning by the sound of "angel-like voices" singing their morning praises. The front door is locked at 23.00 each night.

The monastery of Profitas Elias

Dating from the early eighteenth century, this monastery crowns the mountain of the same name at the top of a long, winding concrete road leading up from Pyrgos. The monastery is widely described as being open to the public and having a splendid handicraft museum but today's visitors are permitted only to see the inside of the small church, while the museum remains locked. As the exhibition is described as well worth seeing, perhaps it will be moved to the new museum building completed in Fira. Unfortunately, the outside of the monastery has its effect ruined by two enormous television transmitters and various military installations that seem to jostle it for position. The view, however, is spectacular and I sought out a soldier to get permission to take a photograph or two. (The area is covered in signs telling you that photography is not allowed and I have no wish to see the inside of a Greek prison.)

Akrotiri

Akrotiri, a very small village on the south coast of the island, receives many thousands of visitors each year who either independently, or as part of a guided coach tour, come to view extensive excavations that have revealed a complete town dating from 2000BC. Although completely surrounded by corrugated iron walls and roofing, the area is well illuminated and maps explaining the features are dotted about the rope-lined route. Some of the explanatory signs are placed in the middle of wooden bridges that you are instructed not to pause on, so some practice at reading as you walk is helpful!

Although much still remains to be excavated, full-time work ceased in 1974 after the death of the project's founder, Dr Spyros Marinatos who, at the age of eight-four, fell from a height of less than a metre and was unlucky enough to hit his head on a stone. In the summer holidays, archaeology students continue the work for two months of each year. Open daily from 08.45 to 15.00 and 09.30 to 14.00 on Sundays. Entrance 300drs and 150drs for students. If you desire the services of a guide then you must go with one of the coach tours.

Wine tasting

If you visit Akrotiri either to see the archaeological site or to soak up some sun on the red or the white beach, be sure to take time to wander up into the village where, after a few hundred metres, there's a building painted with the proclamation that wines of all kinds are available for tasting and sale.

Manolis Arvanitis and his two brothers continue their father's work of both barrel-making and wine-production, They used also to distil *souma* and *ouzo* until the customs officials put their seals on the stills. The huge vats inside the cellar contain wines dating from 1956 and of all types, from a very dry white to what, for my sweet tooth, is sheer ambrosia: a "black" wine that is so thick it leaves colour behind on the glass if you swirl it! Manolis likes to explain his theories on the therapeutic properties of his wines and, with the aid of a well thumbed phrase book, you will soon be made to realise that nothing short of a miracle lies within each glassful. He has a supply of plastic bottles to fill for those who wish to buy some of the produce, but it must be transferred to a glass container as soon as possible as both the wine and the plastic start to deteriorate rapidly.

Wine tasting at Exo Gonia A village on the road to Kamari holds a nightly festival in season where, having paid a set fee in the travel office, you may taste as much wine as you like while enjoying the displays of Greek dancing.

Ancient Thira

Just outside Kamari and from the far end of the sea front road in
Perissa are signposted routes to Ancient Thira. After twenty-six
hairpin bends on its zig zag course — the first two and the last eight
of which are concreted, and the remainder of very uneven
cobblestones with the occasional pothole right on the corner for fun
— you reach a parking area where, if you can still walk, a mobile
canteen sells refreshments nearby. Two hundred metres of "goat-
defying" track later, you reach the boundary of the area; the fact
that there is no entrance fee is small consolation for having
completed the endurance test. After a further 300 metres, you arrive
at the first of the unintelligible signs: the Greek lettering has been
translated into the Roman alphabet but the meaning of the words
hasn't. The site is full of ancient rocks, sand and stone blocks plus
more rocks, sand and stone blocks. Wherever you see a bored-
looking young man sitting inside a roped off area, you will know
that somewhere nearby there is something of great significance! I
thought the sun had affected the poor fellow who told me that the
rock face behind him held murals of a dolphin, lion and the artist's
head, and I gave him a very sympathetic look before he stabbed
various places with a finger and, sure enough, with this further
instruction I could just make out the appropriate shapes.

Maybe I lack imagination, but I found nothing there to dispel the
feeling that I had been conned up that horrendous road, and I felt
resentment of the damage done to my suspension (yes, I mostly
refer to the bike) and nervous system. It made matters worse when
I got lost and couldn't find the way out, finding ropes barring my
way on all four sides with nothing to indicate which side of the rope
I was supposed to be on. The site is open from 08.45 to 14.30
Monday to Saturday, 09.30 to 13.30 Sundays; closed on Tuesdays.

Carpet weaving school, Fira

The school is next door to the Dominican Convent and well
signposted as far as the door, which is not inscribed. Less than a
dozen young girls are at present employed at the school but there
is a sense of great industry as their fingers fly, completing knot after
knot, cut after cut, all much too fast for you to make out the
technique used, even when they slow down to half speed for your
benefit. The finished products are sent to the mainland for sale
although carpets of a similar type are sold in Fira.

The activities of the National Welfare Organisation are destined to improve and educate young people and extend all over Greece.

Handicraft schools in general and those of carpet making in particular aim at:
1. Keeping young people in morally healthy and family surroundings.
2. Improving living conditions of the Greek people and helping peasant families increase their income.
3. Preserving the tradition of popular Greek arts.

Pupils may apply for a post in the school after their elementary studies, i.e. from thirteen years on. They must attend school until they learn the craft well and then each receives a loom as a gift and twenty kilograms of thread so that she may weave a carpet for her own use.

Our carpets are embroidered in knots in the Persian way and their quality depends on the number of knots per square metre.

DOLONIC	18/20*	36,000	knots/sq.m.
MACEDONIA	24/24	57,000	"
MYSTRAS	24/31	74,400	"
PELLA	28/36	100,800	"
IONIA	35/35	122,500	"
KNOSSOS	44/50	220,000	"

* (That is twenty lines in length and eighteen knots in breadth per ten centimetres.)

The output of a well trained pupil is about 7,000 to 13,000 knots per eight hours of work.

Reproduced from a notice displayed in many languages within the carpet-weaving school, Fira.

(Above) *View over the whitewashed houses of Fira town towards the southern tip of the island.* **(Below)** *Fira is perched on the precipitous rim of the caldera, high above the harbour (which can just be seen at the bottom of the picture). (Photos R. J. Thomas)*

Day trips

The various travel offices in Fira offer a large selection of day and half-day trips both by coach and boat. There are also weekend cruises that call at Paros, Mykonos and Naxos. Choices are (in brief):

- One day cruise to Folegandros, Sikinos and Ios with an option for pre-arranged delayed return of from two to four days.
- One day cruise to Amorgos, or Ios, or Anafi.
- Akrotiri coastline: volcano, hot springs, Thirasia and Oia.
- Volcano and hot springs.
- Full day coach trip to Akrotiri, Profitas Elias, Perissa (refreshments and leisure stop), wine tasting in Fira.
- Akrotiri and Profitas Elias.
- Panayia Episkopi, Mesa Gonia, Pyrgos, Imerovigli, Skaros, and Oia to watch the sunset.
- Evening wine tasting in Exo Gonia.
- Ancient Thira: three departures and returns daily. No guide.

Roller-skating

Perissa has a roller-skating rink facing the beach.

Skaros

This is a huge jagged rock from the top of which you can enjoy the most spectacular of all views of the island and caldera, so long as you have a sufficiently good head for heights to complete the hour-long walk.

Beaches

Santorini has a number of agreeable beaches to offer, most of which are black. These are some, going around the island clockwise, starting at Oia.

The Vaxedes are along the north coast, where the low rocks give way in many places to small sandy stretches. While providing seclusion, these little beaches are very exposed to the elements, and litter from passing ships and possibly other islands tends to collect there. This long stretch is reached by the concrete road that leaves Oia, and a few cafés and snack bars are dotted along the route.

The concrete surface soon gives way and long before **Gialos Karteradou** (the nearest beach to Fira) is reached, you are on a dirt track which has many climbs and descents, and its deep sand can easily get you stuck with your wheels spinning. As far as **Monolithos** there is a continuous narrow sandy beach with signs here and there asking you to refrain from nudism as the area is enjoyed by families. Two tavernas and two cafés are found 300m south of the enormous tomato puree factory and in the same area some shade is provided by a thin line of trees that edge the sand.

Kamari and **Perissa** are both long black sand beaches, dotted with pedaloes and closely packed with bodies in the summer months. All facilities are just across the roads that verge them both.

From Perissa to Akrotiri the area is criss-crossed with dirt tracks leading to tiny hamlets and attractive, isolated beaches. Here and there a disused tomato processing factory keeps a lonely vigil.

On the road to Perissa is a primitive signpost pointing right and reading "Surfers Front Line". I followed the road that led past eight derelict windmills and then another that ended at an incredibly remote taverna but could find no trace of this promised delight. Two English lads were just ahead of me on a moped when I came to the taverna and, as I reached the top of an incline, I was horrified to see one jump off and the other just manage to stop the bike on the gravel strewn slope, inches from a sheer drop!

Akrotiri has two notable beaches: Red Beach and White Beach. The former is signposted from the main road and a restaurant nearby has named itself "Red Beach Taverna". This however is deceptive as the only red there is the colour of the geraniums and the cliff face behind the satanic black rocks on the shore line. At the end of this "beach" is a little church on a promontory and a path, indicated here and there by daubs of white paint, ascends and leads round to Red Beach proper, which is a fifteen-minute walk away and requires flat shoes and a head for heights, but proves well worth the effort. Built into the rock face is a minute taverna that has been converted from an old boat shed and here the man from the ticket office at the excavations sells his homemade wines.

At the end of the asphalted road in Akrotiri is a small stony beach, a fish restaurant and a jetty where caiques leave to take passengers to White Beach. This 500 drachma, thirty-minute return trip, is the only way to get there. A small and very white pebbly beach awaits you and the scenery passed en route is quite spectacular.

Santorini, Akrotiri — Kokkino Ammo (Red Beach). The tiny taverna built into the cliff base is just visible on the far left.

Back at Oia again are **Armeni** and **Armoundi** beaches. Both have very small patches of sand and pebbles and most people prefer to swim from the rocks. The paths down to these beaches from the town are stepped and steep so be sure to save enough energy for the ascent at the end of the day!

Thirasia, Nea Kameni and Palea Kameni

Barring gales, boats leave daily from the port below Fira to embark on the many variations on the tour around the caldera. Some round the point at Akrotiri and take in the fantastic rock formations, other visit **Aspronisi** (White Island) and there are varying lengths of stay at all the ports of call.

Nea Kameni (New Burnt) is the island where the volcano still shows some signs of activity and steaming sulphurous gases escape from gaps in the rocks. If you enjoy the smell of rotten eggs then the long uphill hike over loose stones will be worth your while.

Palea Kameni (Old Burnt) is a smaller islet where the boats don't dock, but those who have remembered to bring a swim suit can either jump over board or ease down the step ladder and swim to shore where the hot springs will reputedly restore any aches from the trek you made to the volcano.

Thirasia, the largest of the four islets, is the stop for lunch and five restaurants line the pebbly beach in wait for the arrivals in the tiny port. Here I found a dish I had not encountered before and was told it is a Santorini speciality; Psefto Keftedes will be translated for you as "Tomato meat balls", but it isn't — the name means "False meat balls", and the ingredients are tomatoes, onions and flour. The result is very tasty.

If you have allowed enough time before the boat leaves again, at the far end of the beach there is a stepped path which leads up to the main village of the island, also named Thirasia. Here the little streets and houses form one of the most delightful villages I have seen in Greece. The tiny church of Agios Konstantinos has gone one better than the usual white and blue exterior decor, and with the addition of pink, yellow, green and red, looks like something out of a fairy story. The same is true of some of the houses whose multicolour schemes are gorgeous. No matter which trip you have taken, there won't be time to explore the island's other village Potamos, but you may have just enough left to enjoy a cool drink at one of the two café/tavernas before heading back down.

For those who wish to arrange a stopover, there is a room-to-rent sign in the village. I would supply more details but there was no-one home when I called. The island is reputed to have no vehicles but this is not true as I saw a pick-up truck on the edge of the southernmost path. The land to the west is much flatter than you might expect from the cliff face that is your first impression of the island as you near the port. I was sorry to leave Thirasia but the boat was waiting to make the trip to Oia where a very brief stop broke the return journey to Fira.

Cable car After this fairly strenuous day it was a great relief not to have to climb the stairway back up to the town or impose myself on one of the dejected looking donkeys that ply the route. The cable car is of Swiss design and the cars take thirty-six people and leave every 20 minutes. The fare is 350 drachmas (or 200 for Greek Nationals). The first run is at 07.00 and the last 20.00 hours. This service does not operate between the end of October and the beginning of April each year. The station is well signposted in Fira town and the large Teleferique sign marks the entrance from the port.

Historical background

Because Santorini is an island of continuing changes, much has been researched and written of its geological as well as social history. When the enormous land mass of Aegis sank to leave what we know as the Aegean, Santorini existed only as a small group of tiny islets protruding from the waves. At this time there was no volcanic activity in the area and the difference in composition between the rock at Monolithos, Profitas Elias and Athinios to that of the rest of the island is obvious even to the untrained eye.

The first volcanic eruption occurred some 80,000 years ago and was massive. Ash must have blackened the sky as molten rock rushed to the surface of the sea to form a roughly circular island once cooling was completed. It was named "Strongyle" meaning round, by its inhabitants in 2000BC. These people were remarkably civilised and lived in two-storey houses, cultivating the land, keeping sheep and extracting oil from olives. Their artwork is of particular note both in the use of colours and the skill of the potters.

This civilisation was doomed, however, as a further eruption in 1450BC wiped it out. It is thought that the cooling gases from the first eruption had left a bubble-like hollow under the surface of the island, and the subsequent volcanic activity fractured the upper surface causing eighty four square kilometres to vanish beneath the waves, leaving only Thirasia, Aspronisi and what we know as Santorini above the surface.

The effect of this collapse is beyond the scope of the human mind to imagine as a tidal wave 250 metres high, travelling at a speed of 350 kilometres an hour, drowned the entire Minoan civilisation of Crete. The dramatic end to this culture and its high level of advancement has given rise to the theories that claim Santorini to have been the site of the lost city of Atlantis.

The island that remained was beautiful and lured Phoenicians to form colonies in 1300BC on what they named "Calliste" which means "most beautiful". The Phoenicians were joined by Dorians from Sparta, and cities, temples and harbours were built. The name of the Dorian leader gave the island its alternative name: Thira.

Between 198BC and 1950 there were fourteen eruptions and gradually the caldera became more shallow and the islets of Nea Kameni and Palea Kameni were formed. The 1707 eruption was recorded in great detail by Tarillon, who tells that it lasted for over a year and that many strange manifestations terrified both the locals and their Turkish overlords who had visited to collect taxes. The very sky seemed to be on fire and huge glowing boulders were thrown into the air to land incredible distances from their source. The air was filled with suffocating and foul-smelling gases and the noise was so loud that two people couldn't hear each other shouting even at very short distances.

The last disaster to hit the island was an earthquake in 1956 when Santorini became famous through its misfortune and help arrived from all corners of the world. The reconstruction brought electrification and altered the type of housing used by the islanders, who left their subterranean *skafta* and began living in the conventional style of dwellings.

Santorini has known numerous masters, all of which, with the constant attacks by pirates, diminished the population which fell to as low as 300 people at one time. Having refused to take their side during the Peloponnesian War, the island was overcome by the Athenians, who were ousted by the Ptolemies of Egypt during the first century. The Macedonians, Romans, Byzantines, Venetians, Spanish mercenaries and, of course, the Turks, all subsequently occupied the island that fortunately today sees a more friendly invasion — the seasonal influx of tourist visitors.

(**Above**) *Like many churches on the island, this one near Oia has a barrel-shaped roof to help withstand earthquakes.*
(**Below**) *The picturesque village of Oia on the northernmost tip of Santorini lies directly opposite the island of Thirasia. (Photos R. J. Thomas)*

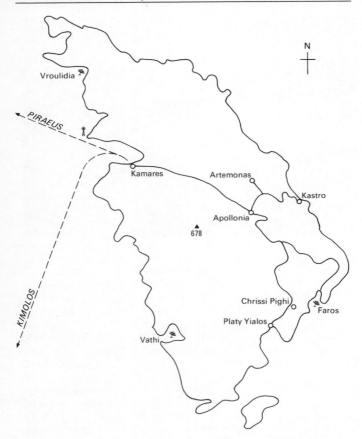

N

Vroulidia

PIRAEUS

KIMOLOS

Kamares

Artemonas

Kastro

Apollonia

▲
678

Chrissi Pighi

Faros

Platy Yialos

Vathi

SIFNOS

Scale 1:135 000

0   5 km

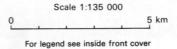

For legend see inside front cover

SEVENTEEN

Sifnos

Population: 2,000   *Highest point: 680m*
Area: 75 sq. km.   *Hotel beds: 280*

Throughout Greece the souvenir shops sell ceramics from this island, so I had imagined that Sifnos was large and both highly industrialised and commercialised. This is not the case. Many of the potteries have closed, perhaps because of competition from the larger concerns on the mainland, and although some of the little side streets in the main town bulge at the seams with visitors, it hasn't yet developed into a resort island.

The first thing you will notice about Sifnos, even as you approach by ferry, is how green it is, and near its rocky coastline the amount of vegetation far exceeds usual Greek island standards. The hills and valleys between the port and the town are verdant even at the end of a long dry summer and this setting shows to greater advantage the brilliant white of the houses, dove cotes and tiny churches dotted amongst the terraces. If the land was flatter, a tremendous amount of agricultural development would be possible. Because of the lushness of the scenery, it is another surprise to learn that in Kastro, the island's ancient capital, there is a shortage of water and it has to be supplied to the villagers by lorry load. Despite its problem this village is one of the most attractive I have encountered and it is a delight to wander through its little streets.

Sifnos is well blessed by sandy, tree-lined beaches that so far aren't overlooked by an abundance of hotels or rooming houses.

Arrival by sea

Sifnos is well served by ferries in all seasons and barring winter storms, there is at least one arrival per day at **Kamares,** its port. The vessels used are of two sizes: one car ferry of standard size and a smaller ship that has room for approximately twenty vehicles. It isn't uncommon for them to both arrive on the same day and it is worth considering, when planning a departure, that the larger vessel has a much shorter journey time and is more resilient to rough seas.

The *Marguerita,* a small passenger-only carrier, leaves daily for the nearby island of Paros at 11.30 and departs from there to make the return at 16.00. The journey time is three hours. It runs from May to end of October. Routes from Sifnos are:

- Piraeus, Kythnos, Serifos, Sifnos.
- Sifnos, Kimolos, Milos.
- Sifnos, Milos.
- Sifnos, Milos, Syros.
- Sifnos, Paros.

Tickets can be purchased both in the port and Apollonia.

Road system

The roads throughout the south of the island are asphalted and in a good state of repair. The only thing lacking is a road of any kind to Vathi, so a trip by caique is needed to reach it, but this has probably helped prevent it being spoilt by development. The roads to all the villages are well signposted.

Buses There are four routes served by new and comfortable buses:

- Artemonas, Apollonia, Kamares.
- Artemonas, Apollonia, Platy Yialos.
- Artemonas, Apollonia, Kastro.
- Artemonas, Apollonia, Faros.

Departures for all destinations are at least hourly and the timetables are displayed in all travel offices and many cafés.

Taxis The island has two taxis and at least one meets all boats.

Petrol Just for a change, there is no problem about finding petrol on the island. Apollonia has two stations, one as you enter the town via Kamares and the other as you leave on the Faros road.

Vehicle hire Both cars and motorbikes can be hired in Kamares and Apollonia. In Kamares, the port area is dotted with advertising signs for this facility but in Apollonia it is less conspicuous; take the road that leads to Faros and the shop is ten metres before the petrol station and on the opposite side of the road.

Maps I found three maps on sale in the souvenir shops; one in the form of a long rolled up piece of paper provides entertainment as you try to decide how to fold it up. The map is clear and accurate but the printing is only in Greek. Of the remaining two, the one with a flower scene on the front is totally unintelligible owing to gross over-enthusiasm when putting in the lines to show the elevations! The map of preference shows a sunset on the cover and this has photographs and information on the reverse side. There is also a small brochure for sale.

Accommodation

As with most islands, Sifnos gets a shortage of beds in the peak season but, judging by the amount of new buildings going up in the port, it is doing its best to meet the demand.

Hotels	Category	Tel.	Beds	Location
Apollonia	B	31490	18	Apollonia
Flora	B	-	14	Chrissi Pighi
Platy Yialos	B	31224	38	Platy Yialos
Kamari	B	31641	35	Kamares
Anthousa	C	31431	12	Apollonia
Korakis	C	31703	20	Kamares
Artemon	C	31303	44	Artemonas
Sifnos	C	31624	19	Apollonia
Sofia	C	31238	22	Apollonia
Stavros	C	31641	28	Kamares
Benakis	C	31334	28	Platy Yialos

Rooms In Faros, Vathi and Kastro this is the only type of accommodation available and many houses display notices advertising vacancies.

Camping Camping is permitted only at the site in Platy Yialos, which is signposted to the right just before the hotel at the far end of the coast road. After turning, it's a further 150m up the track and to the right. The new site has all the facilities.

Where to eat

Sifnos doesn't have a lot of eating places to choose from but amongst those it has are some very good restaurants. In Apollonia, Thanassis at "Krevatina" is an adventurous cook. In Kamares, as well as the fast food businesses, there is an inconspicuous taverna

on the sea front road, recognisable by the small booth-like ticket
office to the left of its front door. Here the food is excellent and
very much in the style of Greek home cooking.

There is no taverna or restaurant in Chrissi Pighi but the Hotel
Flora cooks for its guests. All other villages have at least one place
to find a hot meal — and don't forget Kastro and Artemonas to
widen the selection. Vathi has two tavernas and a fish restaurant.

Nightlife

At the moment there are surprisingly few places to choose from to
go for an evening's entertainment. In Apollonia there's the
Andromeda Disco 100 metres further uphill from the petrol station
on the Faros road. The Marguerita Disco is 150 metres from
Apollonia on the Kastro road. The pastry shop under the Anthousa
Hotel shows videos every evening and the films are usually in
English.

*Sifnos. The main street in Kastro where the occupants of the
little houses, painstakingly paint the edges of the stones that line
the street.*

What to see and do

Ceramic studios

In Kamares, there are still two shops on the sea front that make ceramics on the premises and you can watch both the throwing and dipping processes. If you wish to take a sample home they both have a large selection of their produce on display and for sale. Made from local clays, the ceramics are distributed to shops throughout Greece.

Museums

The island has two museums, one archaeological and one folk. The latter is found in the square in Apollonia and opens from 09.00 to 15.00 Monday to Saturday. The archaeological museum in Kastro is still being completed but the informal setting of the various marble engravings, statues and pottery fragments makes a refreshing change from the uncomfortable silence that imposes itself in many such establishments. Here you have to be careful not to step on anything and the attendant will gladly stop work from mending his nets long enough to tell you anything you wish to know about the exhibits, as long as you speak Greek of course! No admission fee will be charged until the work is finished. Opening hours are as for the folk museum. It is signposted from the main path in Kastro.

Kastro

This village was the ancient capital of the island and it has retained all the charm of a traditional Greek hamlet. It is well worth taking an hour or two to amble around the maze. The little cemetery and the two tiny churches in the valley below are very photogenic, as they contrast sharply with the surrounding greenery.

Trips

As previously mentioned, it is possible to spend one and a half hours on Paros and return the same day. The *Marguerita* leaves from Kamares at 11.30 and returns at 19.00.

Caiques take passengers along the west coast, southwards to Vathi, where you can stay either for a day's sunbathing or for a longer period in one of the rooms to rent. The journey is pleasant and you can wonder at the herds of wild goats leaping surefootedly around the rocky crags as they stare back at you.

Monasteries

Sifnos has more than its fair share of monasteries and they have been built on the most inaccessible mountain tops. Some of the more easily reached are:

Panayia tou Vouno Our Lady of the Mountain is visible from the road to Faros and is 200 metres along a reasonable dirt road. It is no longer inhabited.

Chrissi Pighi Golden Well is well signposted between Faros and Platy Yialos and the road is good except for the last ten metres. The monastery is open to visitors and has a few primitive rooms for the use of people wishing to stay there. Around the low outer wall the steps of the many paths down to the rocky sea edge have been meticulously painted to indicate the routes. Directly behind the church the rocks lead down to a memorial, whose white marble looks very out of place amongst the strange greens and yellows of the native rock.

Monastery tou Vrissi: The Monastery of the Source made a lasting impression on me: the impression was made on my left hand when the enormous door slammed on it. The bruises lasted two weeks, during which time I had to learn to drive my trusty moped one-handed or remain immobile; I also had to enlist the help of a passerby to heave it up onto the stand before I could park. If blame is to be placed, it must surely rest on a dementedly friendly cat who leapt into my arms the moment I cautiously entered the grounds, having received no reply to ringing the bell. Weaving in and out of my feet as I tried to look around the buildings, she was a positive menace until I picked her up again in order to make better progress. At this time a priest appeared and asked me to be sure not to let her out when I left. Well, this was much easier said than done and, having failed to track down the priest to get him to hold her, I had to make a dash for it while growling loudly, which is when the door got me! I can testify that although the grounds are pleasant, they are unspectacular — unlike the door which is three inches thick and would serve well in any bank vault.

Useful information

Health matters If you are reading this chapter in sequence you may already have guessed how I came to find the address of the doctor! Not, however, until after I had been sent on a wild goose chase in five separate directions by various locals. At the T-junction out of Apollonia, take the Artemonas road and just above the turn off to Kastro, a crazy paving stepped path leads up to the left into a walled garden containing a statue. There are X-ray facilities and staff are very helpful. 09.00 to 12.00 Monday to Saturday. Tel. 31315. There are two well signposted **pharmacies** in Apollonia.

Money matters There is a branch of the National Bank of Greece in Apollonia and the usual opening hours are extended in peak season to cope with the exchange transactions. The post office is next door but one to the bank. Open from 07.45 to 14.15 Monday to Friday.

Telephone office The O.T.E. is down hill from the main square in Apollonia and fifty metres from the petrol station. Outside of these opening hours (07.30 to 14.30, Monday to Friday), calls can be made from the pastry shop at the T-junction but with the television working it is difficult to hear and if they are showing football or basketball, forget it!

Sifnos. The white gravestones and the blue church domes of the peaceful cemetery contrast sharply with the lush greenery of the hillside, from where it faces the Kastro, the island's ancient capital.

Centres of population

Kamares

The port of Sifnos is attractive along its seaward edge where brightly painted caiques are moored off the tree-lined shore. Further away from the water's edge, however, the scenery is not so appealing as the modern looking buildings are out of the traditonal style.

This is a popular centre for visitors and all facilities have been provided for them.

Apollonia

Also called "Hora", this is the island's capital and contains the bank, post office, surgery, telephone office, cafés, restaurants, one or two souvenir shops as well as hotels and rooms to rent.

The town is visible from two kilometres away as you ascend the road from Kamares, and it begins as it ends: with a petrol station. Two hundred metres further on, the square is reached. Here the buses stop, but as there is very little parking space everything else has to continue uphill to the T-junction where the roads lead to Artemonas and Faros. The pedestrian-only streets start from the square and the main street curves right and ascends the hillside, before rejoining the road at a spot where a red-roofed windmill has been converted into a house and stands as an unheeded example to two other derelict windmills by its side. This area is known as Emborio and a very good taverna above the windmills makes it worth a visit.

Artemonas

This is a very unusual village because of its layout. Buses deposit you in a long "square" below all the houses and businesses, and from there branch three stepped streets. What makes it different from a typical village is that the main streets haven't been networked with smaller, interconnecting streets and it is possible to walk a very long way before reaching a turn off. To see all the village needs quite a long time.

At the top of the settlement is a converted windmill with a blue roof and used as a taverna, reached from the perimeter road on the right-hand side of the hill.

Kastro
This is a typical unspoilt Greek village oozing with old world charm. The museum and tavernas provide somewhere to pass the time once you have explored all its little alley ways.

Faros
Faros is a small fishing village with a good sandy beach, a few rooms to rent, and tavernas. This area is developing on its outskirts and is clearly intended to become a larger resort to which it is well-suited.

Platy Yialos
This is the furthest resort served by road from Apollonia, and the buildings are all set either side of a road that runs parallel to a long sandy beach. At the far end of the road, a cul-de-sac, are the hotel and a turn-off to the island's only camp ground.

Sifnos. Kamares Beach enjoyed by late season visitors.

Sifnos. Kamares, the island's port.

Vathi

A lovely sight at the end of the hour-long caique trip from Kamares are Vathi's five sandy beaches all backed by trees and interspersed with a few houses and tavernas. The little church of Tahiarhes sits on the water's edge and looks well against the inviting blue of the sea. Caiques leave morning and evening according to demand, and times are posted in both Kamares and Vathi. The single fare is 250 drachmas and well worth it.

Beaches

Undoubtedly the best place for beaches is **Vathi** (see above). All the resorts have good beaches including the port. The only beach not easily reached by road or caique is at **Vroulidia,** in the north, and as this is a very small, pebbly beach, it doesn't get many visitors.

Historical background

Sifnos was once an exceptionally wealthy island owing to the very productive gold mines there. Mythology tells that each year, the people sent a tenth of the gold extracted to the god Apollo in the form of an egg, which was then added to a mounting collection in the treasury at Delphi. One year the islanders decided to send a gold plated rock in place of the usual tribute. In consequence it is said that Apollo allowed Polycrates to fine them heavily and from that time the island became "Sifnos" (empty) as the mines sank below sea level.

Sifnos was colonised by Phoenicians, Cretans and Ionians and before the island fell to the Turks was ruled by the Kozandinis of Kythnos, who had allied in marriage with the Venetian Da Koronia family.

SIKINOS

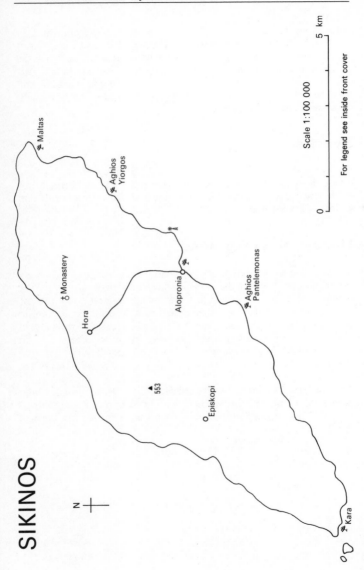

Scale 1:100 000

For legend see inside front cover

EIGHTEEN

Sikinos

Population: 300   *Highest point: data unavailable*
Area: 36 sq. km.   *Beds: 152*

Small, rocky and barren, Sikinos receives few visitors but is obviously expecting this situation to change since construction work in the port is extensive and the skeletons of new houses compete with the project of building a jetty for earliest completion. The port expansion will not only take the bother out of getting on and off the ferries by means of caique transfer, but should enable easier delivery of food supplies that become scarce at the end of the season. Fresh fruit and vegetables are hard to find.

Unfortunately, the same enthusiasm that has prompted the building of new accommodation hasn't been applied to maintaining the aesthetic value of the island. Large amounts of sand have been removed from the beaches to use in road-making that will surface the existing dirt road from the port to the village. Some beaches have already been denuded and the port beach is at present suffering attack.

For the moment at least, the port is no one's idea of a beauty spot but the island is partly redeemed by a very pretty village which is its only settlement, set high on an inland peak.

As you may have gathered, a large proportion of the local population are construction workers, and most of the remainder are receiving a retirement pension.

Sikinos was once noted for the quality of its wines and today a very palatable rosé retsina is produced by many households.

Arrival by sea

It isn't any easier to get to this island than it is to disembark at its port, Alopronia, once you have arrived. In season, there are three arrivals per week from the mainland and one in winter. Sensible shoes should be worn to give you a good grip while walking down the rear door for the transfer to caique. Some ferries set you down by means of a side door at which two or more sailors wait to haul people and baggage aboard and help others disembark. I shared a caique with a cement mixer because after a lengthy and heated argument with the crew of the ferry about whether it was possible to load it or not, and who would put it off at the other end, the islanders gave in and took it back again. The routes are:

- Piraeus, Syros, Paros, Naxos, Ios, Sikinos.
- Sikinos, Folegandros, Santorini.
- Sikinos, Ios, Folegandros, Santorini, Kimolos, Milos, Sifnos, Serifos, Kythnos, Piraeus.

There are also day trips calling at Sikinos from Santorini, Ios, Paros and Naxos.

The caique transfer costs eighty drachmas, which should be paid to the man with the knotted hanky on his head. Tickets are sold on the quayside before departures and at the shop furthest from the sea in the port.

Sikinos. The village is divided into an upper section (shown here) and a lower section, linked by a stepped pathway.

Road system

Three years ago, the islanders decided that a surfaced road was necessary to link the port (Alopronia) with the village (Hora) and so the stone path was torn up and the blasting and levelling began. It hasn't been finished yet which has resulted in financial problems for the over-enthusiastic would-be bus driver, who had rushed out and bought a bus with a bank loan. The road is five kilometres long, steep and gives you false hope in the mistaken belief that once you climb the first hill top, the village will appear; only there is another hill and valley to be tackled before you reach your destination. There are few vehicles on the island, no operating bus or taxi, and no petrol for sale.

Accommodation

There are no hotels on Sikinos but a fair selection of rooms to rent both in Alopronia and within the first kilometre along the road leading from the port to Hora. Hora itself has a few rooms available and information can be obtained in the cafés. The names and telephone numbers of some who rent out rooms are:

Owner	Tel. No.	Beds	Location
Nikos Manalis	51236	70	500m from the port
Yiorgos Manalis	51281	12	500m from the port
Yiannis Halkeas	-	4	Behind the lighthouse
Loukas Manalis	51234	12	Port
Katerina Sigalas	-	8	Port
Flora Marakis	51244	10	Port
Panayotis Koundouris	51232	16	Port
Michaelis Galakis	-	8	Port
Loukas Manalis	51234	6	Hora
Stavros Margetis	51237	6	Hora

There is no official camping ground but many people pitch tents between the trees just behind the port beach.

Where to eat

The most popular restaurant is owned by Nikos Manalis and is situated 500 metres above the port on the left-hand side of the road. The meat and fish are barbecued in the garden nearby and the aromatic wood smoke is a good appetiser.

There is a fish taverna on the water's edge and to the left of the port at the top of a stairway is a family-style restaurant that also serves breakfast and pizzas.

Hora has only one taverna, Kamina, and the cooking and atmosphere are good. In addition, there are two cafés in Hora and two in the port.

Night life

The small "Disco Sikinos" is 400m up from Alopronia.

What to see and do

Episkopi One hour's walk from Hora, very much alone at the top of a hill, sits a church built in the seventeenth century. This well-preserved structure was built around the ruins of another whose purpose is the subject of various theories. Some say that the marble columns now part of the facade of the church belonged to an Apollonian temple, others that it was the tomb of a deified hero. **Zoodohopigis** This monastery is now closed but the key may be obtained from the priest. Ask at the cafés in Hora.

Useful addresses

Money matters There is no bank on Sikinos but the usual transactions are made at the post office, which is one of the first buildings in Hora (0800 to 14.15 Mon to Fri). Foreign currency can be changed at Panayotis Koundouris's shop in Alopronia.
Police The police station is in Hora to the left of the main path as you ascend and down a short flight of steps. Tel. 51222.
Health matters The surgery and pharmacy are next to the church in the village square. Tel. 51211.

Telephone office The O.T.E. is between the post office and main square in Hora. Open from 07.45 to 14.15 Monday to Friday. Panayotis Koundouris has a metered phone at his grocery in Alopronia.

Centres of population

Hora

The village is theoretically divided into two sections and named Kato Meria and Epano Meria: Lower Part and Upper part. A stepped stone path wanders between the houses and the traffic is an almost continuous stream of donkeys and mules laden with firewood to stock up for winter fireplaces and cooking stoves, above which the terracotta chimney stacks are the only deviation from the all white, cuboid houses.

There is a small square in the centre which provides an attractive setting for a *cafeneon*. Its large pine tree gives shade from the sun whose strength seems intensified as it reflects from the white walls.

Many of the buildings have been abandoned and some have been bought and renovated by foreigners which, according to the definition of the locals, includes Greeks from outside the island. The sale of property has now been regulated as it was feared that prices would be driven up to levels prohibitive to young local couples seeking a first home.

Beaches

Sikinos has a dearth of beaches and those it has are largely pebble. The situation has been aggravated by the removal of sand to use in cement making.

Maltas, in the north of the island, is a small sand and pebble beach reached by a two-hour walk or hired caique. **Alopronia** beach, in the port, has a reasonable amount of sand at the time of writing and rocks edging the bay provide an alternative for those who enjoy diving. **Kara** on the southern tip is mostly rocks with some sand and pebbles, as is **Aghios Pantelemonas,** forty minutes walk south of the port. Perhaps the best beach is **Aghios Yiorgos** to which a caique departs in the morning and returns in the afternoon to the port. Here a 200m long sandy beach is found at the base of a steep rocky valley. The one house may open as a taverna some time in the future.

Appendix A

The Greek language

The main reason for including this chapter is that the effort of learning a few words of the language will be repaid many times by the reception you will get from the Greek people. Just to wish an islander "good morning" in his language is like paying him a compliment and although he may then assume that you speak fluent Greek and proceed to rattle on at top speed, you will be instantly accepted and liable to some of the very generous Greek hospitality.

Some of the smaller islands have very few English-speaking inhabitants and so a few of the most commonly used expressions may be helpful but a phrase book is a worthwhile investment and this chapter does not aim to replace them.

All Greek words in this book are spelt phonetically and not in the accepted English equivalent spelling. The syllable stress is very important in Greek and to put it in the wrong place can change the meaning completely. The accent denotes the syllable to be stressed.

The alphabet

The Greek alphabet is confusing because some of the letters that look like ours have a totally different sound:

A α alpha	apple		Ξ ξ ksee	rocks
B β veta	never		O o omikron	on
Γ γ gamma	yellow or gap		Π π pee	paper
Δ δ thelta	then		P ρ roe	roe
E ε epsillon	enter		Σ σ sigma	sand
Z ζ zita	zip		T τ taff	tiff

H η ita	ch<u>ee</u>se	Y υ ipsilon	pol<u>i</u>ce
Θ θ thita	<u>th</u>ong	Φ φ fee	<u>f</u>end
I ι iota	p<u>i</u>ck	X χ hee	lo<u>ch</u>
K κ kappa	<u>k</u>ind	Ψ ψ psee	syna<u>ps</u>e
Λ λ lamda	<u>l</u>ink	Ω ω omega	<u>o</u>n (or owe
M μ mee	<u>m</u>other		at the end
N ν nee	<u>n</u>ice		of words)

There are numerous letter combinations that make unpredictable sounds but this is rather off-putting for the beginner and so if you think you are ready for them, it is time to buy a teach yourself book.

Some conversational gambits

Meanwhile, it is useful to be able to form a few elementary questions and make one or two simple statements. Apart from ensuring your basic survival and comfort when there is no one around who speaks English this will, as said before, create a really friendly rapport with the local people.

The following lists will help you to put a few simple sentences together. Of course, these will not be in grammatically perfect Greek (a language cannot be learned so easily) but if you say them carefully they should be comprehensible to any Greek person, who will be absolutely delighted by the effort you have made. Remember to stress the accented syllables.

List A — basic statements and phrases

Yes: *neh*
No: *óhee*
Please/you are welcome: *parra kallóh*
Thank you: *efharistóe*
Good morning: *kallee máira*
Good evening: *kallee spáira*
Good night: *kallee níhta*
Hello/goodbye: *Yássoo (yássas* is more formal)
Greetings: *hyéretay*
Where is: *poo eénay*

I want: *thélloh*
I am: *éemay*
You are: *éesthay*
He/she is/there is/they are: *eenay*
We are: *ee már stay*
I have: *éhoe*
You have: *éhetay*
He/she/it has: *éhee*
We have: *éhoomay*
They have: *éhoon*
I don't want: *then thélloh*

Now if you turn to lists B, C and D you can add words to some of these to articulate your needs or ideas. Statements can be turned into questions by putting an intonation in your voice — to change "you are" to "are you?", for instance

List B — accommodation

hotel: *ksennoe doheé oh*
room: *thomátteeoh*
house: *spéetee*
bathroom: *bányoh*
shower: *dóos*

bed: *krevártee*
hot: *zéstee*
cold: *kréeoh*
blanket: *koo vérta*

List C — getting about

far: *makree áre*
near: *kondá*
bus: *leo for éeoh*
taxi: *taxí*
ferry boat: *férry bott*
street: *óh thos*
road: *dróh moss*
corner: *go neár*
left: *arist erráh*

right: *thex ee áh*
single: *applóh*
return: *epist rofée*
ticket: *ee sit ée ree ah*
post office: *tahee droh mée oh*
laundry: *plind éereeoh*
bank: *tráp ezza*
telephone: *telléfonoh*
petrol: *vrin zée nee*

List D — eating and drinking

restaurant: *eest ee at
    ór ee oh*
food: *figh eet óh*
coffee: *kaféh*
tea: *ts ígh*
breakfast: *proh ee nóh*
sugar: *záh harree*

salt: *a lár tee*
pepper: *pip áir ee*
wine: *krass ée*
beer: *béerah*
water: *nair óh*
without: *hórris*
oil: *lárthee*

List E — other useful phrases and words

As you gain a little confidence — and begin to understand the replies you get — you will probably be able to make use of the following phrases and words — when shopping, for instance. Note that, although days and numbers have been given here, it is more difficult to talk about time, such as the hours of boats and buses, so that is when you ask for it to be written down!

I want this: *thélloh aftóh*
I don't want this: *then thélloh aftóh*
What time does it leave?: *tee óra févyee*

What time does it arrive?: *tee óra ftáhnee*
Please write it down: *moo toh gráps etay parra kallóh*
Excuse me/sorry: *sig nóh mee*
I am an Englishman/woman: *éemay ángloss/angléeda*
Please speak slowly: *méelet ay argár parra kallóh*
Don't!: *mee!*
Go away!: *féev yet ay!*
Help!: *voh ée thee ah!*

Monday: *theftéra*
Tuesday: *tréetee*
Wednesday: *tetártee*
Thursday: *pémptee*
Friday: *parraskevée*
Saturday: *sávatoh*
Sunday: *kirree akée*

one: *énna*
two: *thé oh*
three: *trée ya*
four: *téssera*
five: *pénday*
six: *éxee*
seven: *eptá*
eight: *oktoé*
nine: *enay yáh*
ten: *théka*
eleven: *én theka*
twelve: *thó theka*
twenty: *ée cosee*
thirty: *tree ánda*
forty: *sarránda*

fifty: *pennínda*
sixty: *ex índa*
seventy: *ev tho mínda*
eighty: *ovthónda*
ninety: *en en índa*
one hundred: *eka tón*
two hundred: *thee ak ówsee ah*
three hundred: *track ówsee ah*
four hundred: *tétrak owsee ah*
five hundred: *pént ak owsee ah*
seven hundred: *eptak ówsee ah*
eight hundred: *okt ak ówsee ah*
nine hundred: *enyak ówsee ah*
thousand: *hill eeyá*

Appendix B
Wind Force: the Beaufort Scale*

B'fort No.	Wind Descrip.	Effect on land	Effect on sea	Wind Speed knots	mph	kph	Wave height (m)†
0	Calm	Smoke rises vertically	Sea like a mirror	less than 1			-
1	Light air	Direction shown by smoke but not by wind vane	Ripples with the appearance of scales; no foam crests	1-3	1-3	1-2	-
2	Light breeze	Wind felt on face; leaves rustle; wind vanes move	Small wavelets; crests do not break	4-6	4-7	6-11	0.15-0.30
3	Gentle breeze	Leaves and twigs in motion wind extends light flag	Large wavelets; crests begin to break; scattered white horses	7-10	8-12	13-19	0.60-1.00
4	Moderate breeze	Small branches move; dust and loose paper raised	Small waves, becoming longer; fairly frequent white horses	11-16	13-18	21-29	1.00-1.50
5	Fresh breeze	Small trees in leaf begin to sway	Moderate waves; many white horses; chance of some spray	17-21	19-24	30-38	1.80-2.50
6	Strong breeze	Large branches in motion; telegraph wires whistle	Large waves begin to form; white crests extensive; some spray	22-27	25-31	40-50	3.00-4.00

7	Near gale	Whole trees in motion; difficult to walk against wind	Sea heaps up; white foam from breaking waves begins to be blown in streaks	28-33	32-38	51-61	4.00-6.00
8	Gale	Twigs break off trees; progress impeded	Moderately high waves; foam blown in well-marked streaks	34-40	39-46	63-74	5.50-7.50
9	Strong gale	Chimney pots and slates blown off	High waves; dense streaks of foam; wave crests begin to roll over; heavy spray	41-47	47-54	75-86	7.00-9.75
10	Storm	Trees uprooted; considerable structural damage	Very high waves, overhanging crests; dense white foam streaks; sea takes on white appearance; visibility affected	48-56	56-63	88-100	9.00-12.50
11	Violent storm	Widespread damage, seldom experienced in England	Exceptionally high waves; dense patches of foam; wave crests blown into froth; visibility affected	57-65	64-75	101-110	11.30-16.00
12	Hurricane	Winds of this force encountered only in Tropics	Air filled with foam & spray; visibility seriously affected	65 +	75 +	120 +	13.70 +

* Introduced in 1805 by Sir Francis Beaufort (1774-1857) hydrographer to the Navy

† First figure indicates average height of waves; second figure indicates maximum height.

INDEX